Creating
Meaningful
Change

A Timeless Leadership Path to
Transforming the Modern Work Culture

Foreword by Ashley Goldsmith,
Chief People Officer, Workday

MICHAEL MORRISON, PH.D.
CLINT KOFFORD

Publishing services provided by Archangel Ink | archangelink.com

Paperback ISBN: 978-1-950043-49-1
Hardback ISBN: 978-1-950043-50-7

Dedications

If the world had just one more leader like Kerry Morrison,
we would be OK.
–Mike

To my wife, Nancy, who has inspired meaningful change in my life.
–Clint

Praise for *Creating Meaningful Change*

"Mike Morrison and Clint Kofford created an easy-to-understand connection on how essential creating, cultivating, and catalyzing change is to great leadership. A must read for both aspiring and seasoned leaders."

— Michael Ehret, Global Head of Talent Management, Johnson & Johnson

"As Mike and Clint reveal, change is inevitable, meaningful change is not. This book artfully illuminates the timeless path of meaning-making that is at the heart of true leadership. *Creating Meaningful Change* challenges us to think about how we can better lead organizations and create meaning that drives change."

— Garry Ridge, Chairman & CEO, WD-40 Company

"This book is a transformational practical guide for life, leadership, and work. The authors, both practitioner-scholars, show that success in leadership is about driving change to get results and providing a path that stems from an inner core—one of meaningfulness—while also having the ability to do what it takes to get it done (including learning from failures). Bravo for a wonderful book that is filled with "aha" moments of insight, examples, conceptual maps, and case studies, making it an effective manual for driving meaningful change."

— Raghu Krishnamoorthy, Director, Penn's Chief Learning Officer Executive Doctoral Program and former CHRO, GE

"*Creating Meaningful Change* really resonated with me! It is timely, smart, and insightful and represents a core message every leader should embrace to be truly effective."

– Jim Loehr, Renowned Performance Psychologist and co-author of the *Power of Full Engagement*

"In this practical, compelling book you will be reminded just how important it is to move beyond our habitual hyperfocus on achieving targets and results, and consciously attend to *how* we reach our goals."

– Annie McKee, PhD, Bestselling Author of *How to Be Happy at Work: The Power of Purpose, Hope and Friendships*

"Simple. Practical. Compelling. Helpful. These are words that describe the new book *Creating Meaningful Change*. In an era where any act of leadership has become increasingly complex, nuanced, and high-stakes, more progressive frameworks, better tools, and a more holistic way to develop is needed. This book gets us to the starting line and gives us all a path to be better and more fulfilled."

– Dr André Martin, Advisor, Board Member, and former CLO of Mars, Nike, Target, and Google

"Clint and Mike created something truly helpful here for leaders and aspiring leaders—a blueprint for driving meaningful change. The concepts and exercises in this book aren't a checklist. They're dynamic and will help leaders at all levels of an organization address key challenges, including finding meaning and driving purpose-driven outcomes for their organizations."

– Rachel Romer Carlson, CEO & Co-Founder, Guild Education

"*Creating Meaningful Change* has inspired me to be more intentional about leading rather than managing. The meaningful change framework is simple but powerful and resonates with my experience in trying to create change. I will be referring back to this book often."

– Brigitte C. Madrian, Dean, Brigham Young University Marriott School of Business

"This book becomes available at the perfect time, as we embrace a new life after the pandemic. Pairing thoughtfulness and leadership, it is a strong reminder to look beyond the power of leading and instead focus on why we lead. Only then will we make great change."

  – Jennifer Hark Dietz, CEO, People Assisting the Homeless

"Creating Meaningful Change provides a valuable roadmap for leaders to recapture the true essence of leadership—at a time when it is needed most."

  – Eric Roza, Chairman, CrossFit

"Mike Morrison and Clint Kofford deliver a powerful look into the perilous void attendant to strict outcomes-obsessed organizational leadership. Especially with the pandemic-driven dispersal of employees and new "remote" and "hybrid" employment philosophies, leaders must strive harder than ever before to establish a meaning-driven work culture. Success invariably hinges on deep values alignment, space for employee and leadership voices alike, and conscious balance between addressing individual needs and elevating team cohesion and accomplishment."

  – Paul Vandeventer, Founder, Community Partners

"Mike and Clint hit the nail on its head. Without purpose, change is just something that either happens or is shoved through. Leading change requires emotional and intellectual shared purpose."

  – Ara Ohanian, CEO, NETSTOCK

"A powerful three-part guide for leaders looking to drive meaningful change for their organizations and the people within them."

  – Bernie Jaworski, Peter F. Drucker Chair, Claremont Graduate University

"In *Creating Meaningful Change*, Morrison and Kofford present a refreshing and contemporary view of effective leadership for teams and organizations. Rather than a rigid "check the box" framework, it focuses on important individual and team introspection, leading to permanent, positive, and organization-wide change. I loved it!"

  – Gary Crittenden, former Chief Financial Officer, Citigroup and American Express

"As long-time friends and colleagues, Mike and Clint have been two of the most influential people in my career and life. As fan number one of Mike's first book, *Leading through Meaning*, I am thrilled that Mike and Clint have collaborated to provide the type of deep yet practical insights required for the extraordinary time we live and lead in."

> – Greg Pryor, Former Senior Vice President, People & Performance Evangelist, Workday

"What will resonate long after finishing this book is the holistic idea that building dignity and meaning should emanate not just from your leadership but from your entire life. In building meaning for others, you build it for yourself."

> – Dr. Nigel Paine, author, mentor, consultant, and broadcaster

"Practical and straightforward guide that simplifies and demystifies the recipe for making change stick: make change meaningful. This should be required reading, not just for leaders but for all change agents."

> – Keith Keating, Senior Vice President and Chief Learning Officer, Archwell

"In a post-pandemic world, meaning has never been more important in the workplace. This book provides a practical and powerful model for how leaders can create the purpose-fueled contexts so many employees are seeking from their organizations."

> – Rob Cross, Edward A. Madden Professor of Global Leadership at Babson College and best-selling author of *Collaboration Overload*

"An absolute must read for any leader aiming to successfully deliver and inspire transformational change! Creating Meaningful Change makes the complex simple, laying out a framework that enables one to quickly zero in on the true meaning behind any organizational change program and how to make it a success. Even more compelling is the insight offered on how we, as leaders, are also changed as a result of the transformation experience and the significant opportunity we all have to help others find a deeper sense of meaning and purpose in life through their role in the change journey."

> – Aisling Cribbin, Chief People Officer, Glanbia Performance Nutrition

"In such extraordinary times, successfully navigating change has never been more perilous. Morrison and Kofford offer a fresh perspective to enable us to voyage through uncharted territory by engaging in a process of wayfinding, sensemaking, and self-discovery. *Creating Meaningful Change* is a must read for any voyager."

> – Michael J. Arena, former Chief Talent Officer, General Motors, VP at AWS, and author of *Adaptive Space*

"In a world that has seen unprecedented change, understanding ways to define and unlock meaningful change for yourself, your team, and your organization has never been more important. *Creating Meaningful Change* provides a powerful framework that is a worthy read for any leader craving to unlock fulfilment and performance with change that matters."

> – Jaime Head, Chief Digital & Technology Officer, Ocean Spray Cranberries

"Now more than ever, people are questioning the purpose of organizations, their ethics and values. *Creating Meaningful Change* helps leaders understand why it matters and gives a practical guide to put their purpose into action. A timely and worthy read."

> – Angela Mangiapane, President, Mars Global Services, Mars, Inc.

Contents

Foreword

In their book, *Creating Meaningful Change,* Mike and Clint reveal an essential truth that *change is inevitable, meaningful change is not.* That revelation could not be more timely.

Already living through one of the most challenging times in generations, our global community faced a catastrophic pandemic and geopolitical instability that created new levels of disruption and chaos. Many lost loved ones or faced sudden economic uncertainty. Thousands of businesses, especially the small ones that enrich our communities, were shuttered. Meanwhile, those living in the U.S. grappled with urgent cries for social justice. Few people were left untouched by these events.

More than the logistical challenges, my colleagues and I at Workday felt a deep personal responsibility for the wellbeing — physical, mental, financial, and career — of our thousands of employees (what we call Workmates) around the world. We felt an equal responsibility to support our customers, ensuring that the critical finance, HR, and planning systems we provided would enable them to operate in a highly uncertain environment. Without precedence (and very little time), we had to make decisions that would impact the collective welfare of the Workday community and beyond.

As just one example, Workday's senior leadership team gave a one-time payment — equivalent to two-weeks' pay — to the majority of employees to help cover unexpected challenges. This action, which may have been surprising at first to some people outside of the company, was later applauded. The extra care for our Workmates translated into extra support for our customers and their millions of employees at a time when it was needed most.

Now more than ever, the nature of leadership and the challenge of change is evolving before our eyes. Leadership today requires a new level of humanity that is well beyond the historic table stakes.

During my professional career, I've had a front row seat to two very successful high-growth companies with founders and leadership teams that operated as both the poets and plumbers that Mike and Clint explore so thoughtfully in this book. While the leaders in each of these organizations had the requisite skills for the job, they also possessed the leadership qualities for creating meaningful change.

I began my HR career at The Home Depot where two co-founders, Bernie Marcus and Arthur Blank, transformed an industry and created an iconic brand. Central to the company's extraordinary success was a corporate culture that valued decentralized management and decision-making, entrepreneurial innovation, and employee commitment and enthusiasm.

In many ways, my experience with transformation, growth, and leadership at Workday resembles that of The Home Depot.

Founded in 2005 by Dave Duffield and Aneel Bhusri, Workday felt a calling to change the world of enterprise software by leveraging cloud technology, empowering users, delivering unparalleled customer service, and providing a people-first workplace. A compelling sense of purpose ensued, cultivating a collegial and values-driven culture that earned Workday a spot on *Fortune's* 100 Best Companies to Work For list in 2015. Unfortunately, it wouldn't be long before we hit an inflection point and our ranking would fall. Positive customer referrals fueled a flywheel of growth that started to dilute our special culture.

It was a moment of truth that couldn't be handled through traditional communication channels. We swiftly engaged leaders and influencers, and used data to test and learn about where we needed to act. We then brought together all people leaders from across the globe to hear from EVERY member of the senior leadership team on why and how our people, values, and culture are at the very center of our success and need to be at the very center of our collective attention. After an intensive and deliberative effort, we saw marked improvement in our measures of business success, including employee engagement, and Workday was honored to be recognized by *Fortune* as a top-five place to work for two years in a row, in 2019 and 2020.

That period in Workday's history served as a great test — of our leadership, priorities, and values. It also prepared us to face new and unexpected challenges. Indeed, I believe that foundation gave us the courage and capability to navigate the events that unfolded in 2020 and beyond.

While I wish I had this book as a timely resource for the pandemic, it has served as a powerful framework for understanding what we just experienced. Its simple "leading change" framework is built around the timeless practices of *wayfinding, sensemaking,* and *self-developing.* Facing the unprecedented change requirements of COVID-19, we were continually having to *find our way* forward, *make sense* out of things (like how we can best connect with each other), and *continue to grow* ourselves (despite the uncertainty that surrounded us). Mike and Clint simply and beautifully illuminate the "how" in these three practices.

They also reveal how it is our meaningful change efforts that create the greatest opportunities for us to grow individually and collectively. Change *is* the new normal and can't be avoided. Consider this book to be a personal guide for evolving your identity as a "change" leader.

The final chapter on "everydayness" reveals how the day is the "best container" to live our lives as leaders. The message is poignant. Beyond the grand strategies and big ideas that we envision, it is what we do each day — over and over — that will create the change we desire. They also offer this simple truth. While leading change can feel like something we manage for others, *nothing changes until we do.*

Prepare to change.

Ashley Goldsmith, Chief People Officer, Workday

Preface

When you entered the eighth-floor auditorium of the University of Toyota, on the wall to your left were just three words:

Create Meaningful Change

It was there for a reason. This simple mantra, posted in the early 2000s, was a gentle reminder to balance the dominant nature of Toyota's continuous improvement culture with larger, more impactful initiatives. While "continuous improvement" was the secret sauce to Toyota's lean thinking philosophy of waste removal, its incremental nature inhibited the meaningful change required in a dynamic marketplace. But that was only part of the problem.

The other challenge at this time was that Toyota in the United States was experiencing growing pains. We were enjoying incredible success and profitability in the marketplace. We were the darling of the business press, and our products were widely praised in the industry. Each month seemed to produce a new sales record. While that was good for the bottom line, this incredible success caused us to overlook some shortcomings in our customer service efforts (in an industry not known for its customer focus).

As a founder and dean of the University of Toyota, it was my hope that it could help broaden Toyota's meaning-making efforts beyond achieving sales targets. (The University of Toyota was a corporate university that provided training and development for our employees, dealers, and suppliers.) The "create meaningful change" meme was central to that effort and was one of the key strategies integrated into our leadership development efforts. A supporting book, *Leading Through Meaning*, was published in 2003 to both capture and promote the process within Toyota and with our University of Toyota external clients and beyond.

Leading through meaning also became the central tenet of my own life as a leader. This has not been an easy journey for me. There have been times over the last two decades when I have lost confidence in our collective capacity to lead and serve beyond our own personal interests as both individuals and organizations. I have lost heart when I failed to aspire to the meaningful change that was desperately needed. But these low moments have not equaled the force of good leadership I have witnessed. Although often hidden or suppressed by other factors endemic in the cultures we work within, the potential for transformation is within us. This book will equip you with the knowledge to achieve it.

During this period, a demonstration project with the United States Olympic and Paralympic Committee was being facilitated by the University of Toyota. Clint Kofford (co-author) was a member of the United States Olympic and Paralympic Committee, and our collaboration sparked an ongoing friendship and partnership that has culminated in this book. Clint's "leadership development–centered" career has taken him from the United States Olympic and Paralympic Committee to Mars to Nike to Johnson & Johnson, where he currently holds a senior talent role. In our collaborations along the way, the pursuit of meaning in our work lives was always at the center of the discussion.

Two years ago, Clint and I decided to meet weekly in an effort to update the original *Leading Through Meaning* book with all that we had learned over the fifteen-plus years since it was published. At the heart of this multi-year effort is both a new book and our three-word definition for leadership:

Creating Meaningful Change

We will show how these three words get to the heart of what it truly means to lead. We will also show how meaningful change is achieved though the timeless and natural practices of *wayfinding, sensemaking,* and *self-discovery.* Much of our writing took place in 2020 and 2021 in the throes of the pandemic. As we emerge from this life-changing period, we believe that *Creating Meaningful Change* will be a timely and valuable resource as we make sense out of *what we do* and *who we will become.*

Onward,

Mike Morrison
May 2022

Introduction

Change Is Inevitable. Meaningful Change Is Not.

At first blush, the concept of meaning may seem too broad to be addressed in the context of leadership. But meaning is essential to virtually all realms of human activity, and leadership is no different. Neither celebrity nor success nor even happiness can rival the life-giving power of meaning. We are constantly searching for it and when it is not present, life—and work—become dull. We also see it most clearly in the paradoxical nature of failure and loss and how those experiences can redirect our lives in some unexpectedly positive ways.

Meaning has the potential to transform us.

There is no better place to start than with John Gardner's definition of meaning. It is a framing that inspired us for more than a decade and still resonates with us today. Gardner was Secretary of Health, Education and Welfare under President Lyndon Johnson and a strong advocate for citizen participation (founding Common Cause).

He is probably best known for his passion for leadership and his inspiring writings where meaning is a central theme, and he eloquently defines it below:[1]

"Meaning is not something you stumble across, like the answer to a riddle or the prize in a treasure hunt. Meaning is something you build into your life. You build it out of your own past, out of your affections

*and loyalties, out of the experience of humankind as it is passed on to
you, out of your own talent and understanding, out of the things you
believe in, out of the things and people you love, out of the values for
which you are willing to sacrifice something. The ingredients are there.
You are the only one who can put them together into that unique pattern that will be your life. Let it be a life that has dignity and meaning
for you. If it does, then the particular balance of success or failure is of
less account."*

Gardner's words inspired many people. In one memorable inci-
dent, Gardner received a letter from a Colorado father who lost his
20-year-old daughter in an auto accident. The grieving man told
Gardner that he found Gardner's moving quote tucked inside her
wallet, and it pleased him to know such sentiments were held near to
her heart.

> *When we are no longer able to change a situation,
> we are challenged to change ourselves.*
>
> –Viktor Frankl

To fully grasp the power of meaning at the personal level, we turn
to Viktor Frankl, founder of logotherapy and author of one of the
most widely read and translated books in the world, *Man's Search for
Meaning.* After enduring the misery of Nazi concentration camps (he
was the only member of his family to survive), Frankl developed a
theory that as humans, we are all motivated by something called a
"will to meaning."[2] Frankl universalized the concept of meaning by
showing how our desire to secure it is essential to being *human.* It can
be simply characterized as:

Living a purposeful life.

It is through this search for meaning that individuals can endure the most extreme forms of suffering.[3] A wonderful example is Frankl's reflections on his wife, Tilly:[4]

We stumbled on in the darkness.... . The accompanying guards kept shouting at us and driving us with the butts of their rifles.... . Hiding his mouth behind his upturned collar, the man marching next to me whispered suddenly: "If our wives could see us now! I do hope they are better off in their camps and don't know what is happening to us." That brought thoughts of my own wife to mind. ... my mind clung to my wife's image, imagining it with an uncanny acuteness. I heard her answering me, saw her smile, her frank and encouraging look ... I understood how a man who has nothing left in this world still may know bliss, be it only for a brief moment, in the contemplation of his beloved.

Tragically, Frankl's wife ultimately perished in the camps. But the indefatigable drive to keep her in his head and heart as he weathered the torments of the Holocaust provided some measure of meaning, of purpose, that kept him going when other prisoners lost the will to live. Meaning enabled him to survive and formed the basis for his entire approach to life. But Frankl provides this warning: "One should *not* search for an abstract meaning of life."[5] In other words, Frankl believes that meaning should not be pursued as a goal in itself. It must be a side-benefit of pursuing goals and aspirations that connect you with something beyond yourself. That is not always easy to do in a world that tends to overemphasize our own happiness and personal success as measures of a life well lived.

That is not to say that happiness is a fool's errand. Like meaning, the pursuit of happiness is also one of our most central motivations in life.[6] Happiness is tough to define, but most of us probably don't require a precise definition anyway: we know it when we feel it, and we often use the term to describe a range of positive emotions, including joy, contentment, and gratitude.

Still, the things that tend to get the most attention in our achievement- and consumption-focused cultures are things like money, status, job promotions, beautiful homes, and lavish vacations, even though we know that the relationship between these things and happiness is elusive. For example:

> *We desperately seek a promotion at work, one that we believe will bring us happiness in its prestige and enhanced compensation. Somehow we are convinced that this new job will change just about everything in our life for the positive. Soon after receiving the promotion, the increased responsibility, pressure, and hours actually detract from our life satisfaction. The anticipated new levels of happiness never materialize. We may even start to wonder if the trade-offs are worth it.*

This suggests that the path to a fulfilled life is not as clear cut as it may seem.

What, then, is the answer?

The exercise in the box below is a simple word-association game. Most people strongly equate "what makes me happy" with the "good life" and the things that we believe will make us happy. In the exercise, participants typically report things like rich family life, great relationships, secure and satisfying work, freedom to pursue interests, opportunities to travel. You get the idea.

Pause and Reflect: Happiness vs. Meaning

Take a few moments to think about the things that make you *happy* (as you define the term).

Next, compare these things with experiences that have brought great *meaning* to your life.

How are they *different*?

Interestingly, when we ask our workshop participants *what experiences have brought great meaning to your life*, the responses concentrate around how one has prevailed over significant challenges or the lessons learned from a major setback. The simple use of the word *meaning* elicits compelling stories or moments of truth in the face of adversity. Some of the stories started as follows:

> *We were about to lose everything we worked for ...*
> *Against my advice, she stood up to the bully ...*
> *It was a moment of truth in our relationship as he headed toward the door ...*

As Frankl discovered, it is our capacity to shape meaning in service to something larger than ourselves that makes life worth living.[7] We have all experienced those transformational moments when we are called into service in some special way. It might be a family member who needs help weathering a crisis. Or a major challenge at work that calls us to bring to bear our full range of skills, including ones that haven't yet been tested. It is often in these unique situations—moments of crisis, challenge, or uncertainty—that meaning comes to life most. It is situations like these that can help us to realize that ...

We are at our best when we are needed.

In our journey together, we will see how it is meaningful change that has the power to transform both *what we do* and *who we are*.

To better understand this transformative power, let's take a closer look at our three-word definition for leadership: *Creating meaningful change.*

The verb "creating" reinforces the open and exploratory spirit wherein leadership thrives. Leading transformation is much less about deciding and influencing and much more about facilitating, bringing to life, making new, inspiring, and building. The change we seek is "meaningful"—connecting us to a worthy purpose that will not only inspire new ways of thinking and acting but grow our sense of self in a positive way.

Creating meaningful change also frames leadership as a *practice*, not a position. It is less about who has authority and more about who is committed to the change we seek. It is less about expertise (and experts) and more about running experiments that deepen our insights. It is less about directing others and more about involving them. It is less about who we are (and our status in the hierarchy) and more about who we want to become. The question we ask gets to the heart of leadership:

What is the meaningful change you are creating?

When we pose this question to leaders, it usually makes them pause.

While they know they are involved in a range of change initiatives, it is the word "meaningful" that gets their attention.

The very word "meaningful" has a powerful, almost magical ability to shift our intentions beyond the urgent requirements of our job to a focus on a larger purpose. The word opens up grand vistas that are often unseen in our work lives. In the discussion that follows, we will show how the path forward is illuminated by three core practices— *wayfinding, sensemaking,* and *self-developing,* with each providing its own unique source of meaning:

Wayfinding	A purposeful direction
Sensemaking	A sense of knowing
Self-Developing	A growing identity

We will show how these elements drive our meaningful change efforts, allowing us to grow individually and collectively. It also begins with this simple truth:

Nothing changes until we do.

If we don't evolve our identities as leaders, the organizational culture will become stagnant and conformist. Instead, the work environment must be a place where we get to shape, question, and affirm who we are and who we want to become. The bottom line is this:

We all want to work in a place where we can find purpose and meaning. If we don't feel this special connection to the organization, we won't trust it to be a place for our personal growth, and we will naturally withhold our commitment and the unique contributions that come with it.

A Final Reflection

This book is neither comprehensive nor technical by design. We simply don't need another overly prescriptive or detailed leadership guide. Rather, our intent is to allow you to hit the reset button and discover anew the centrality of meaning in your leadership life. Our purpose is to provide a new and simple framing that *inspires* more than prescribes.

While we will emphasize learning by doing, we also know that learning by experience alone is not enough. We hope that *Creating Meaningful Change* will provide you with the necessary mental models, supporting strategies, and motivation to increase your capacity for leading. Where appropriate, we layer in relevant theoretical foundations that complement practical framings that enable *wayfinding, sensemaking,* and *self-developing*.

Each chapter will also be an opportunity for you to reflect and begin the necessary inner work. The ability to toil in thought and to ruminate deeply has become a lost art in today's go-go world. That is why this book is written in the form of a personal inquiry. Reflective questions, simple templates, and thought-application exercises will assist the reader in integrating the concepts into their own meanings.

(Note: To keep the book succinct and focused on the central message, we will provide the reader free access to our website where you can continue the learning with additional insights, timely articles, and more. Please see www.meaningfulchangebook.com.)

Let's begin.

Chapter Overview

An Introduction to Each Chapter of Our Journey

Chapter One: Leading through Meaning

Leadership is *creating meaningful change*. We explore how *meaning* is central to this definition and examine how it shapes our lives, fundamentally changing *what we do* and *who we are*. We will reveal its far-reaching impact on our well-being and its dramatic impact on the nature of work. We also discover how elusive meaning can be in our work lives.

Chapter Two: Wayfinding

Wayfinding is about direction and progress and explains how meaning often lies not in the destination but in finding our way as we embark in new directions. We reveal the "journey-like" nature of the change process, traveling from one place to another. The place we travel *from* is a condition or state that no longer serves us. The new place we are traveling *to* is worth all of the challenges because it reshapes our purpose in dramatic ways. We will show how this simple "FROM-TO" framing creates the tension required to energize the change journey.

Chapter Three: Sensemaking

Sensemaking is an exciting capability that can transform us. It takes us beyond traditional problem-solving efforts that rely too much on yesterday's solutions. We also align sensemaking to the guiding principle of *thoughtfulness,* bringing a special character to our ongoing explorations.

Chapter Four: Self-Developing

The essence of our self-development efforts is best revealed through our ME-WE development paths. The ME path is inward and focuses on the personal side of leadership. The outer WE path is where we find our place in the world as we learn to serve beyond our own needs and aspirations. We do this collaboratively, with and through others.

Chapter Five: Everydayness

We believe the day is the perfect container for managing our challenging and fragmented organizational lives. We will show how *everydayness* brings the necessary stability and sustainable progress to our meaningful change efforts. It is important to remember that most transformations take time and require an ongoing purposefulness that becomes the best part of our days.

The Journey Forward

We offer some final reflections and encouragements for the ongoing journey, including an invitation to continue the discussion at www.wechangefirst.com.

Appendix One: Examples of Wayfinding Journeys

Four case studies from various industries and organizations that serve to broaden and build on the lessons of the book.

Chapter One
Leading through Meaning

The Art of Making a Difference

In the West we tend to think of leadership as a quality that exists in certain people. This usual way of thinking has many traps. We search for special individuals with leadership potential, rather than developing the leadership potential in everyone. Through all of this, we totally miss the bigger question: "What are we, collectively, able to create?"

—Peter Senge

Key Themes	Questions We Will Answer
Plumbers and Poets	*Why are both roles essential to our success?*
Leading through Meaning	*What makes change efforts meaningful?*
Three Timeless Practices	*What are the three timeless practices for creating meaningful change?*
The Meaningful Change Framework	*What is the overall territory we will be covering?*
Other Change Frameworks	*How does the Meaningful Change Framework compare to other popular frameworks?*

Plumbers and Poets

A memorable framing for leading and managing is James March's metaphor of "plumbers" and "poets." Both roles are required of all leaders.[8] The plumbing work relates to the "managing" side of our roles. It includes the creation and updating of systems and making sure things work well. As plumbers, we want things to "flow" and not get "backed up." We add new "piping" where necessary but much of our work is attending to ongoing maintenance. (We love the connection of this metaphor to the lean thinking concepts of value, flow, and removing waste!)

The "poet" work, or the leadership part of our roles, is focused on creating meaning. Historically, poets have been the truth tellers in society who actually saw beauty and redemption in all of the failure, setbacks, and doubt that we experience individually and collectively. When we embody the role of poet, we are trying to reawaken the spirit and sense of purpose that can be overcome by the busyness of organizational life. In other words …

> *… we are trying to summon the courage and candor that has been dulled by the necessary routine of our regular work.*

The "plumber" in us walks into a meeting with an agenda to get things done. The "poet" in us looks to inspire and encourage the heart. The work of the plumber gives us a sense of progress, helping us to build momentum. The work of the poet is about shaping positive identities for the group, a kind of holding space where we not only grow individually but become deeply connected to the meaningful change we seek.

Without good plumbing, our execution and implementation will suffer. After all, managing capabilities is what allows us to "operationalize" our change efforts, creating the necessary stability and predictability in our organizations. Without the "poetic" side of leading, we will not achieve the deeper connection to our work and each other.

Ultimately, while both roles are indispensable, it is the poet that embodies the leadership approach of…

Creating Meaningful Change

Creating meaningful change is enabled through three core practices:

Wayfinding
Sensemaking
Self-Developing

We start by getting our arms around how natural these practices are—especially in our everyday lives. For example, we may have to literally "find our way" to a new restaurant where we are meeting a friend. We have not had this cuisine before, so we "make sense" out of the menu and ask our server a few questions to help us in our selection. We actually love the new dishes, "self-developing" and expanding our palette and capacity to try new things. The wayfinding, sensemaking, and self-developing never stops as we navigate our days and our biggest challenges.

Many of us who descend from immigrants have ancestors who leveraged these three practices in carving out a new life. For some, it was finding their way to a new country with expanded opportunities. They would have to adapt and make sense of their new surroundings as they grew their identity and capabilities in new ways. It is these same human-centered practices that allow us to make the shift to the meaning-making mindset that leadership requires.

The 2020 pandemic stimulated a meaningful change response. We went into *sensemaking* mode as the crisis unfolded and the questions kept coming:

> *How do I keep myself and my family members healthy?*
> *How can I reliably acquire food and other necessities?*
> *My boss seems to be taking this lightly; what can I do?*

As things stabilized a bit, the sensemaking led to *wayfinding* as we began to ask, which way do we go now? Imagine a local restaurant owner who wants to not only stay in business, but also to serve the food needs of her patrons. A new purpose emerges as she tells her employees:

We need to go in a new direction. We are now a food
pantry—with pick-up and delivery services.

Few people were left untouched by the far-ranging, life-changing challenges of the pandemic. Many lost loved ones or faced sudden economic uncertainty. The resulting wayfinding and sensemaking were often motivated by our most dominant instinct, survival. And with all of the uncertainties thrust upon us, we weren't always at our best. We could be impatient, over-reactive, and lacking empathy for the plight of others.

But as we adapted, many of us also found new sources of meaning as we tried to find our way forward. Beyond developing a new daily rhythm in our lockdown existence, we learned some important new things about ourselves. Under very challenging conditions, we found new directions and goals (wayfinding); figured out how to get there (sensemaking); and developed a stronger, more capable sense of self along the way (self-developing).

It is worth putting these *meaningful change* practices into a side-by-side comparison with *managing* to reveal their unique and distinct natures. The "explorative" nature of these meaningful change practices certainly aligns to the role of "poet" in our leadership efforts.

	Managing "Plumber"	Meaningful Change "Poet"
What are the core practices?	Planning Directing Communicating	Wayfinding Sensemaking Self-Developing

Managing has a firm logic to it. It makes sense. What could make more sense than *planning*? Managing is best symbolized by rational thinking or our *head*. Creating meaningful change feels totally different. It requires a deeper kind of thoughtfulness characterized by the heart. Meaning-making focuses on interpretations, judgments, and emotions. It draws upon our emotional intelligence and is best captured by the question:

How do we "feel" about something?

Unfortunately, it is these natural meaning-making processes that tend to be underrepresented in the leadership development process.[9] That is understandable given the general fixation on outcomes.[10] Unfortunately, this results-orientation limits the kind of meaning-making facilitated by the three practices above. As noted in our introduction ...

We tend to be good plumbers.
But we often fail as poets.

We can all probably come up with examples of others in our current and past experience who meet this description. But meaning-making and the creation of meaningful change is what constitutes leadership. We have to look past the role. It is not the position of authority that enables meaning but the meaning-makers whom we look to as our true leaders. In fact, it is most often the group participating in meaning-making efforts that creates the necessary leadership for the situation at hand. In this context, we can see how limiting it is to think of leadership as primarily emanating from a single person in the "leader" or "authority" role.

We will show you how to become actively engaged in the process of *creating meaningful change.* In doing so, you dramatically increase the organization's capacity to grow, not by filling the traditional leadership pipeline but by dramatically increasing its size and diversity. As we noted earlier, it is easy to get stuck in the managing side of the equation. After all, the management challenges of setting goals, organizing the team, and producing results can make us feel like we are leading.

But let's be clear. Without meaning at the center of our efforts, we will most likely fail in three ways:

We fail to learn. In our rush to make some progress, we fail to discover new insights or experiment with new modes of activity that could expand our thinking. We also fail to develop the deeper sensemaking capabilities that are vital to leadership.

We fail to facilitate new identities. One of the great benefits of any change effort is the opportunity to essentially redefine our identity, both individually and organizationally. It's a chance to rethink "who we are" and "who we need to become." The traditional problem-solving approach impedes our personal or emotional connection to the change we seek.

We fail to connect. We fail to deliver the kind of conversation that connects us and builds trusting relationships as we shape new meanings. As a result, people may know the current status of a project but will lack a sense of shared purpose and commitment.

The Meaningful Change Framework

We will go deep into the three core practices of *wayfinding, sensemaking,* and *self-developing* as our journey together unfolds.

Where are we going? (Wayfinding)
How will we get there? (Sensemaking)
How will we need to grow? (Self-Developing)

The Venn diagram below represents how the different elements of the "meaning-making" system interact. The circles represent the circular and ongoing nature of our learning. The overlapping nature of the circles reveals their synergistic, mutually reinforcing dynamic as the meaningful change process progresses.

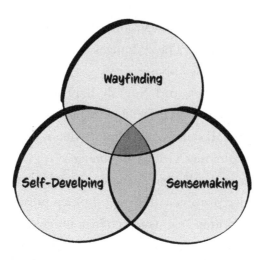

We will fully explore each practice area in the discussion that follows. Their differentiating elements are captured below.

Meaningful Change Framework			
Practice Area	*Source of Meaning*	*Guiding Principle*	*Motivating Tension*
Wayfinding	A purposeful direction	Purposefulness	Betweenness (FROM-TO)
Sensemaking	A sense of knowing	Thoughtfulness	Not knowing (Thinking-Acting)
Self-Developing	A growing identity	Authenticity	Self-determined vs. Belonging (ME-WE)

Other Change Frameworks

Not surprisingly, a wide range of change models have appeared over the years. We will highlight a few of the popular ones while showing how they compare to our own.[11]

Kurt Lewin's influential model of managing change was introduced in the 1940s. This oft-cited three-phase change process starts with "unfreezing" or creating a new vision to guide the "transitioning" to new ways of doing things. These changes are then embedded into the culture in the "refreezing" phase.

David Cooperrider and Suresh Srivastava pioneered the Appreciative Inquiry method to facilitate collaborative, strengths-based, and positive change. It starts with defining what is right about the current system to inspire new visions for change.

Michael Beer and colleagues' six-step model brought more specificity to the change process with its step-by-step prescriptions.

Finally, John Kotter's eight-step change model is one of the most popular. It is well-known for its first step of creating a "sense of urgency" before proceeding.

Change Models: 1940s to Present				
Lewin	Cooperrider & Srivastava	Beer, Eisenstat & Spector	Kotter	Morrison & Kofford
3 phases	4 phases	6 steps	8 steps	3 practices
Unfreeze Transition Refreeze	Discovery Dream Design Destiny	Mobilizing Shared Vision Build Consensus Spread To All Monitor/Adjust Institutionalize	Sense of Urgency Guiding Coalition Create a Vision Communicate It Empower Others Short-Term Wins Consolidate Institutionalize	Wayfinding Sensemaking Self-Developing

We (the two authors) have experienced and have found value in all of these frameworks in our own efforts to navigate change. All frameworks, however, will be incomplete or inadequate in some way. For example, with its focus on the positive and strengths, the Appreciative Inquiry approach tends to miss or minimize some of the problems that derail a change effort. The multiple-step models (Beer and Kotter's) can feel formulaic, overly prescriptive, and like a project that can be implemented with a clear beginning and end. These types of models sometimes feel too theoretical, academic, or abstract, as if they were cooked up in an MBA classroom. They might be intellectually rigorous, but they lack the flexibility and humanity required for a messy, real-world application.

The other challenge is that the nature of our organizational change efforts can vary widely, from major internal reorganizations to complex mergers to ongoing improvement efforts within a unit. The low rates of success and the long time delays for tangible results to emerge highlight the elusive nature of leading change. For these reasons, we identify most with Lewin's approach because it is intuitive and simple, helping people to grasp the complexities of managing change without a lot of buzzwords or confusing steps. It also gets to the heart of why people resist or support change by exploring these invisible forces. But this we know for sure:

When a model continues to be popular and applicable
for almost a century, it is a keeper!

Our model builds on these positives. Not only are the three components straightforward and self-defining/self-evident (e.g., wayfinding is *finding our way*), they capture the essence of what it means to be human (as opposed to playing out some scripted role in the organizational hierarchy). We bookend our model at the opposite end of Lewin's to represent our belief that it is time to come home again to a simpler, timeless approach. Although most change models embed the basic elements of assessing the current situation, creating a new vision, involving stakeholders, and capturing hard-fought gains, we hope to show how our *creating meaningful change* approach adds vital new and human-centered practices that make it worthy of attention.

A Final Reflection

We learn to accept that the exercise of leadership will always be challenging. Any efforts to create change will be beset with failure and characterized by struggle. More than just grit, character, and stamina, it requires a Frankl-inspired belief that it is our human nature to find meaning in the most difficult situations.

The process can be messy and even downright miserable, but the longer arc of our lives reveals that the human spirit and our capacity for meaning-making almost always prevails. In the discussion that follows, we learn how to maintain our integrity despite the inherent dangers of doing so. We learn how *leading through meaning* provides our best chance for an extraordinary life in organizations and communities.

Chapter Two
Wayfinding

The Art of Finding Our Way

I'm not lost for I know where I am.
But however, where I am may be lost.

–Winnie the Pooh

Key Themes	Questions We Will Answer
Change as a Journey	*How is change best captured in the journey metaphor?*
Wayfinding	*What are the leadership elements of finding our way?*
Core Case Study	*What's a great example of wayfinding in action?*

Change as a Journey

The most appropriate metaphor for our "wayfinding" practice is that of a journey or "finding our way" from one place to another. Of course, the "place" we travel *from* is a condition or state that no longer serves us, which is why we're leaving. We believe the new place or condition to which we head will be worth all of the challenges, setbacks, and surprises along the way.

The film *The Wizard of Oz* brings a transformational journey to life as Dorothy and her newfound companions each seek to complete themselves.

Scarecrow wants a brain.
Tinman wants a heart.
Lion wants courage.
Dorothy wants to find her way home.

Of course, that won't be easy, as they have to overcome an evil witch, flying monkeys, and their own limiting beliefs that others (like the Wizard) hold the answer they lack. Ironically, they find that what they were seeking was within them all the time. But you have to leave the comfort of home—put yourself into the world (along with trusted others)—to learn these essential truths.

We can see how Dorothy's journey parallels Joseph Campbell's model of the "hero's journey." Campbell was a scholar and student of myth-making, and he described the hero's journey as the most common story structure, one that has been shared by numerous cultures worldwide for thousands of years (and is still evident in many of our favorite movie plots).[12] In this paradigm, the hero ventures forth, abandoning the comfort of home to undertake a critical, often existential challenge (his life and/or the lives of his family or community depend on him). Facing conflict, adversity, and their own imperfection on the journey, the hero ultimately triumphs before returning home, transformed.

We are often called to journeys that represent the necessary change we want to see in our world. At some point in our lives, we also discover that the journey itself is the most rewarding and soul-serving part of the process, even more so than the moment of triumph. We find that when we do reach our destination—like completing a key work project—we can feel a bit empty until that next meaningful project emerges. In other words …

Deep satisfaction lies not in arrival but in the journey.

The practice of *wayfinding* elegantly captures the journey metaphor. Historically, wayfinding refers to how travelers would navigate their way in finding their destination, especially when the routes were unmarked or unclear. Wayfinding in a modern, day-to-day context means navigating uncharted or challenging destinations in our personal and work lives. There is something very special to being on the way to some important destination. It is the anticipation that keeps us leaning in as we seek out the right path, keeping distractions to a minimum. It is that wonderful feeling of ...

There is some place I need to be.

The first journey is always personal, as we continually shape our own purpose in life, the central and motivating themes that serve as the reason we get up in the morning. It is the inner pull we feel that is impossible to ignore. For some, purpose is deeply connected to their work. For others, their purpose lies in their responsibilities to family and community—or possibly their faith or spirituality. What we know for sure is that "purpose" will be unique for everyone and will undoubtedly shift through life as we evolve from new experiences. Questions of purpose are especially important during periods of transition as we seek to find meaning in these unsettling times.

> *Two roads diverged in a wood, and I took the road less traveled by, and that has made all the difference.*
>
> –Robert Frost

Creating meaningful change taps into these deeper and personal needs for purpose. Most importantly, it is the journey we take together. It answers the question posed by Peter Senge in the quote we shared:

"What are we, collectively, able to create?"

Wayfinding: From, To, and In Between

To fully answer this question, we begin with the wayfinding practice, capturing all of the elements below from our "meaning framework." We will start by showing how the meaning we receive from wayfinding comes from a sense of purpose achieved as we carve out new directions for our organization. We then reveal the powerful tension of "between-ness" we unleash when we create a FROM-TO framing that brings clarity to both our current reality and our vision for the future.

Practice Area	Source of Meaning	Guiding Principle	Motivating Tension
Wayfinding	A purposeful direction	Purposefulness	Betweenness (FROM-TO)

While wayfinding is a natural endeavor, it is a sense of purpose beyond ourselves that brings it to life. Unfortunately, many of the efforts to create a sense of shared purpose can get lost in the operational urgencies of organizational life. In other words, we lose much of the opportunity to involve our team members in something bigger. It is the FROM-TO journey that frames the meaningful change we seek. We start here.

The "FROM-TO" Journey

In simple terms, wayfinding consists of just two elements:

From: Defining current reality in a way that makes it clear that we will need to change.

To: Establishing a vision of the future that captures our new guiding purpose.

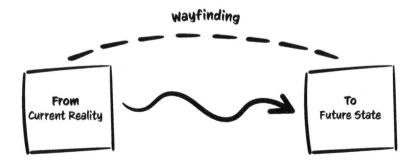

Sadly, much of the criticism aimed at leaders today is the failure to both understand and openly communicate the current conditions impacting the organization (the FROM) and the failure to articulate a future worthy of commitment and our best efforts (the TO). We also know that many organizations are less than candid in their assessment of the current reality. We see it clearly in "spin" or in efforts to impose an "overly positive" interpretation of things. Politicians in office are perhaps the most notorious offenders. But we all do it: exaggerate, over-promise, embellish, slant, skew, promote, push, and position. In organizational life, there is often an expectation that we will "spin" things to frame them favorably. After all, we want our proposal to get approved. Or we want to put the best face on our lagging results.

It is almost guaranteed that in any formal presentation made at work, the truth is skewed.

In our *creating meaningful change* approach, it is truth-seeking about our current reality that empowers us to see things differently. The term truth-seeking also gets at the notion that there is rarely just one truth or that something remains true forever. We bring a truth-seeking spirit to our wayfinding, coming to terms with current reality in the most open and honest way. We ask tough questions:

How have we contributed to our lagging results?
What is keeping us from fully addressing our shortfalls?
What needs to be said?

In the case study below, we will see how CFO Jamie engaged her organization in the kind of reflection and open dialogue that would reveal some painful truths. We will also see how this confirmation of current reality inspired a new and bold vision for the future for their organization. When both the FROM and TO are clearly and passion-ately defined, it conspicuously reveals that our current state no longer serves us, and the future state is the one to which we must aspire. This tension between now and then, here and there, one pole and the other induces a special tension that energizes the change journey.

It is this "betweenness" where the potential for transformation occurs.

"Betweenness" is the ambiguity and disorientation (also known as the liminal state) that occurs when we are between things. Betweenness is also experienced when we have taken on a challenge without fully knowing how it will be resolved. In our FROM-TO journey, it is the uncertain path we venture on as we leave the certainty of our current state. This state has the potential to be both unsettling (because of the uncertainty) and game-changing (because we will have to creatively find a new way forward).

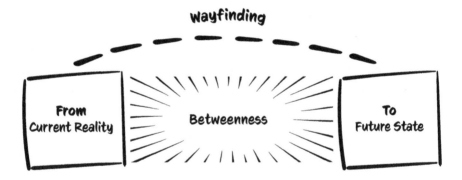

When the nature of the change we seek begins to shape *what we do* and *who we are,* our emotions are elevated. We can become excited or fearful, hopeful or disillusioned. This is one of our critical pause points throughout our journey because many leaders still see emotions as something to be suppressed or managed. Our view is the opposite.

Emotions need to be seen as a fundamental part of any change.

Emotions are a fundamental part of the human experience, and they serve us in our daily life. Anxiety alerts us to potential threats before proceeding with caution. Anger can mobilize us to necessary actions that might be out of our comfort zone. Emotions also help us to interpret what is "truly going on" as we sort through and make sense out of our feelings of fear, anxiety, and excitement.

> *In the universe, there are things that are known, and things that are unknown, and in between them, there are doors.*
>
> –William Blake

Most importantly, emotions signal that we need to rethink and reframe things as we try to create new meanings with our fellow journeyers.[13] In this way, our emotions serve as a vital interruption to the normal, almost automatic nature of our routine work practices. When things get emotional, energy mobilizes and attention becomes focused. It reminds us of the old leadership adage …

… in the absence of a crisis, invent one.

The good news is that we tend to be at our "behavioral best" at work, so people tend to exercise more care before leveraging the special energy that emotions bring. In other words, although disruptive at times, we see a special intelligence in our emotions. To create meaningful change requires an adaptability and emotional intelligence. It's a capability that needs to be developed broadly in the organization. Emotionally intelligent people are simply more aware that this is happening and can choose how they will respond. Brené Brown says it best in her best-selling book *Daring Greatly*:

> *"Vulnerability is not weakness, and the uncertainty, risk, and emotional exposure we face every day are not optional. Our only choice is a question of engagement."*

When we step outside of our routines and comfort zones, the opportunity for personal growth and creativity occurs. Leaders have that critical first conversation with their team to create enough psychological safety to move forward in an open and honest way. Please note that this is not your typical project launch meeting. We are inviting people onto a unique journey and our language and tone should reflect the quality of a special invitation.

We talk candidly about the risks and make a commitment to maintaining an open mindset toward the inevitable new ideas that will occur. We further commit to challenging our own assumptions and beliefs, acknowledging the inevitable biases that we all hold. Finally, we prepare for the failures and setbacks that will certainly occur. In crossing into *betweenness,* we need to create a sense of purposefulness that is often absent in our normal work lives. Yes, we sense risk but …

… we are energized by it.

The following case study demonstrates how it is in the *betweenness* where the transformation occurs. We see how a talented CFO, Jamie, helps her organization get to the heart of what is truly going on and shaping a new and compelling "what should be." This process brings definition to our wayfinding efforts. As the case unfolds we will also see how meaning-making is best achieved collectively as the larger finance organization in Jamie's company participates in these purposeful wayfinding efforts. We are at another one of our important pause points:

*You can't create meaning for others. They have
to find and develop it for themselves.*

At Toyota Motor Sales, USA, the "FROM-TO" framing was used to balance the sometimes limiting focus of an operations-oriented culture.[14] Beyond making things work well through their problem-solving efforts, Toyota managers at all levels were challenged to envision and facilitate larger, more meaningful change efforts. For example, a manager in a call center may seek to transform their outcomes through more customer-centered processes.

Over the last fifteen years, dozens of organizations beyond Toyota and hundreds of leaders have experienced the "meaningful change" process thanks to our coaching and consultative support, often producing transformational results while transforming the leader and participants along the way.[15] Below is a real-life case study of a consumer products organization that we guided through the process.

Case Study: The CFO's Long Drive Home

It all started with the unexpected remarks by the CEO that the finance department was doing more to "prevent sales" than to support them. It was one of those throwaway comments at a weekly leadership meeting. Most of the participants tried to neutralize the comment with some light laughter.

It didn't work. The meeting ended on a tense note.

The drive home that night for Jamie, the CFO, was a long one. She certainly saw some evidence that her group had "overcorrected" in their efforts to rein in costs during a slow-growth period. But that was the challenge they had been given and it wasn't an easy job because many of their cost-containment efforts were highly resisted by the departments, earning them the moniker of "cost police." Although hurt by the CEO's comments, Jamie sensed it was also an opportunity for some soul searching on how to best position her department for the future.

The next day, Jamie pulled her leadership team together to do some initial "sensemaking" around the CEO's comments. While feeling the pressure to react in some way, Jamie also knew in her gut that a true leadership challenge was emerging and couldn't be rushed. With her team huddled around a conference table, she didn't sugarcoat the message from the CEO: "He's frustrated with us and feels that our cost-control measures might have gone too far. The company's leadership team seems to agree." She simply asked, "How do you feel about this?" She then listened for over an hour as the team unleashed some emotional responses:

"Did they forget that we were at the cliff's edge before the cost cutting?"
"The departments lack discipline. They got us into trouble in the first place!"
"We may have saved the company. Anyone mention that?"

Allowing the cathartic flow of responses actually seemed healthy. It allowed the leaders to blow off some steam. However, toward the end of the discussion, a slight shift in attitude started to occur. As hard as it was, the finance leaders were doing their best to understand how this had happened:

"I wish we would have had more time."
"I can understand how the other departments feel. The targets were extreme."
"With the urgency around the cuts, we didn't have much time to collaborate."

As the conversation evolved, they were able to acknowledge how they got "lost" in their efforts to cut costs. They could also see how their "overcorrection" impacted the business and their relationships with the sales and marketing side of the organization. These painful realizations also paved the way for a dialogue on a new way forward. The positive shift in comments provided a nice end point for the discussion. The "FROM" or current state of the change effort was also starting to emerge in an honest and open way.

The next session, occurring just two days later, allowed Jamie to start framing the "TO" or future state. She did so with a simple question for her leadership team:

"Who do we want to become?"

The question initially drew blank stares. The senior managers were anxious to begin rethinking their deliverables and moving beyond the "cost police" label. But Jamie persisted: *"Change is fundamentally about our identity and who we want to become. We can set goals and change processes all day but if we don't change, the new efforts will never stick."*

After a few sessions, the potential for shaping a new identity for the finance team was beginning to emerge. They then decided to hold a series of town hall–type meetings with their respective units to bring the same discussion and truth-telling into the whole organization. In the spirit of openness and candor, the overall questions for the town hall meetings were framed as follows:

How did we become the "cost police"?
What do we want to become in the future?

Acknowledging that previous change efforts tended to be top-down, the meetings were also designed to allow for lots of conversation in small groups. These smaller conversations allowed employees to express their range of feelings, from frustration to hope. It also allowed them to raise questions and concerns while also making suggestions that could be captured and integrated into the larger discussion. Managers were coached and encouraged to proactively respond to local issues when possible. Albeit slowly, meaningful shifts in the change process were starting to occur.

Also, as common "destination" themes started to emerge from the small group sessions, they were played back to the larger organization, motivating even more informal conversations. The "wayfinding" conversations inspired a consensus on becoming more integrated in the business as "more than numbers people" but as trusted business partners. With a future state emerging, the CFO described a coming transformation that the larger organization applauded:

The honest and disarming recognition that they had become the "cost police" created credibility with the larger organization. But now the focus was on the future, the TO state. Jamie knew that it would require more definition and clarity if it was going to shape new thinking and behaviors. But the change journey was now launched, and the organization was entering the challenging but exciting state of *betweenness*.

The next chapter will reveal how the sensemaking practice leverages this tension with learning initiatives that will move the finance organization toward its future state. However, in the appendix we feature four additional case studies (shown in the table below) that will not only enhance your understanding of the wayfinding practice but also reveal a range of diverse application opportunities.

	FROM	TO
Consumer Products Division *Heat from the parent company*	*Buying the Market*	*Customer-Centered Growth*
Hospital Unit *Somebody help!*	*Lone Rangers*	*Happy to Help*
College Prep School *The purposeful school*	*College Admissions Madness*	*Developing Leaders for a New World*
Community Counseling Services *Let's think about this*	*Isolated on Zoom*	*Best of Both Worlds*

A Final Reflection

It is the wayfinding practice of creating the FROM-TO journey that gets to the heart of leadership. It answers the central question we pose:

What is the meaningful change you seek?

We have seen how wholehearted attempts to answer this question can reshape a work culture and its performance in the most dramatic ways. It creates a special focus on what matters most while elevating the status of our work and who we desire to become. It cuts through the meaninglessness that can creep into the meetings, conversations, and communications that often characterize our work lives.

Imagine for just a moment that all leaders were expected to answer this question. Imagine if performance reviews not only addressed our day-to-day proficiency in ours jobs but captured the meaningful change we have created. *Just imagine.*

Chapter Three
Sensemaking

The Art of Thinking Things Through

There's nothing wrong with enjoying looking at the surface of the ocean itself, except that when you finally see what goes on underwater, you realize that you've been missing the whole point of the ocean. Staying on the surface all the time is like going to the circus and staring at the outside of the tent.

–Dave Barry

Key Themes	Questions We Will Answer
Change Management	*Does it work?*
Surviving "Betweenness"	*Why is sensemaking the necessary response?*
Sensemaking	*How does this practice enable our change efforts?*
Learning Initiatives	*How do we bring some needed structure to our sensemaking efforts?*

Change Management

In our estimation, 70% of change efforts fail, and we've certainly had our own experience with a change failure! Even with the guiding assistance of the popular change models we explored in the first chapter, success has been elusive. Before we can fully explore the practice of sensemaking, it is important that we establish some truths about change, especially the transformational efforts that we seek through our three practices.

> *If you want to truly understand something, try to change it.*
> —Kurt Lewin

The first truth is that change surrounds us in our organizational lives. It would be hard to keep track of all the changes going on at our work. New strategies are continuously emerging and improvement initiatives are routinely envisioned (and almost as easily abandoned). Just imagine the number of small changes that individuals or small teams implement without much review. In large organizations, the level of change activity can be quite complex. Heck, even small startups fail under the weight of too much change.

The second truth is that most of us assume that we can effectively manage our change efforts as a rational, step-by-step process (hence the emergence of multi-step change models noted earlier). We go into "project management" mode as we clarify our overall change goals and the milestones to get there. In other words, we believe we have more control than we actually do. This false assumption, more than anything, contributes to the high failure rate of change initiatives. While any change effort will benefit from a project management mindset, true transformational change is more about empowering people than managing them. It is more about including them in the process than just directing them toward outcomes. As we noted before, we can't dictate meaning for others. They need to find and create it on their own.

As we reflect on these two truths, we can see that change in organizations is influenced by just about everyone and controlled by no one. Until there is a culture of sensemaking and an enlightened leadership that understands the collective nature of meaningful change, the failure rate of change initiatives will remain high.

We begin to reshape the transformation process as we enter *betweenness*, the state created by our FROM-TO framing.

Surviving Betweenness

Once we step into *betweenness*, the game changes. We have to switch gears from the rational "I know what is next" logic to immersing ourselves into a state of betweenness or "not knowing." A different sense of being emerges when we deliberately cross into the unknown, opening ourselves up to opportunities we cannot foresee in our normal work routines and our routinized thinking. For many of us that can be challenging.

The reasons are simple. We lose that sense of control when not following some pre-programmed agenda. It feels awkward not having a next step we are moving toward. We substitute this step-by-step familiarity with the practice of *sensemaking* or learning our way …

… one meaningful step at a time.

Without ongoing sensemaking to shape new thinking and innovations, we will merely be tweaking yesterday's solutions. We get stuck in that trap all of the time by keeping one foot in the comfort zone and building on what we already know. It "kinda" works. But the potential to transform *what we do* and *who we are* will not exist. The practice of sensemaking gives us that transformation option.

We will show how sensemaking elevates performance through repeated failures, deeper learning, and ongoing efforts.[16] The "evolving" process of change feels a lot different than the more predictable and controllable work we do within our jobs and the projects we manage.

It is non-linear, overlapping circles of different sizes that best represent the ongoing and emergent learning of the sensemaking process.

We will have to make sense out of "what we do" and "who we are" as we move toward our new purpose or "TO" state.

What we do: *How will our work change in support of our new purpose?*

Who we are: *How will we shape our new identity to fully embody our new purpose?*

The good news is that these questions are almost inseparable. By answering one, you are beginning to answer the other. It's a back-and-forth process. Here's an over-simplified example for a chain of pet stores:

Feedback from customers reveals that the staff are not very friendly. The staff is surprised but accepts the findings and decides they want to be known as the "friendly" pet store. They start by making sense out of the kinds of things they could do to promote friendliness (e.g., always greeting customers upon entry, more on-floor support, free sample treats for their pets, etc.). In the same conversations, they realize that these offerings will fall flat if they are not delivered by a "friendly" associate. Lots of discussion ensues on how they can truly embody a "friendly" way of being.

We are at a pause point. The truth is that most change efforts fail to fully achieve their desired "TO" state. The most common failure, using our pet store example, can be described as follows:

> *While our work has changed, who we are still lags. We know how to do "friendly," but we fail to "be it."*

It is the dance of doing *and* being. The bottom line is that we will always fall short of the meaningful change we seek until we can embody and be that change. It is the practice of sensemaking that facilitates doing these deeper, more personal explorations.

Sensemaking: A Sense of Knowing

Sensemaking provides a "sense of knowing" that brings great meaning to our work. The guiding principle of thoughtfulness infuses our efforts with a special character. Finally, the motivating tension of "not knowing" is what draws us into the core sensemaking practice of *thinking* and *acting*.[17] We will show how it is these small cycles of learning that allow us to close the gap between our current and future state in the most meaningful way.

Practice Area	Source of Meaning	Guiding Principle	Motivating Tension
Sensemaking	A sense of knowing	Thoughtfulness	Not knowing (THINKING-ACTING)

As with wayfinding, sensemaking is our natural response to the complexities and challenges of life. It is more than just problem-solving. *Sensemaking is a deeper process of truly understanding a complex issue.* It gives us the feeling that we are not just reacting to some challenge but thoughtfully responding to it. As noted above, it is *thoughtfulness* that serves as the guiding principle for our sensemaking efforts. Here's why.

In organizational life, there is a clear bias toward decisive, action-oriented leadership.[18] We can understand why, given the pressures for differentiating performance in heartless markets and the competitive nature of our individualistic and achievement-oriented work cultures. In our "just do it" orientation, we also lose sight of others. We communicate with them but don't connect. We inform them but fail to fully involve them. We just don't have the time (or at least it feels that way). Paradoxically, it is through others, through their diversity, that a deeper truth can be revealed.

To fully understand the practice of thoughtful sensemaking, it is useful to get our arms around the word *thoughtful*. First of all, it may not be a word that we typically associate with leadership, which more often connotes qualities like bold, decisive, strategic, and visionary. But there truly is a special quality to the word thoughtful. It suggests an enduring moral quality, a character trait that helps to define the person.

Interestingly, thoughtfulness actually has two meanings—and both point to useful character traits.[19] **Meaning One** relates to the sensemaking or the deeper thinking and discipline we might bring to an issue (e.g., *she was thoughtful in her writing*). **Meaning Two** relates to how we relate to others in considerate or empathetic ways (e.g., *more than kind, he brought a special thoughtfulness to his dealings with others*). It also suggests a sense of compassion toward others. Finally, there seems to be a "permanence" to the word thoughtful, as it usually signifies an aspect of one's personality, not just a fleeting behavior.

But here is the challenge. Although we tend to be overly reactive, it is through action that we learn the most.[20] Our approach shows you how to create the appropriate levels of thinking-acting balance. It is supported by compelling research that reveals how we gain true understanding through small and meaningful actions.[21] An underlying principle is that we won't truly understand a complex situation until we take some action. So, the operative question in sensemaking would be:

*Given the unknowns of the situation, what would be the next
best action that would further our understanding?*

In the 1960s, the father of sensemaking, Karl Weick, revealed how
sensemaking would become increasingly critical in a world where
cause-and-effect relationships were becoming less clear, complexity
was increasing, and uncertainty was the new norm.[22] Sensemaking
acknowledges we don't know what we don't know. It requires patience,
curiosity, and intuition. It also requires running small experiments and
tests, where the real learning occurs. We may start with a basic understanding of the challenge, but we instinctively know that the solution
will take some time (and most likely some experimentation) to tease
out a viable path forward.

We learn to complement our insanely human speed of thought
with the uniquely human pacing of thoughtfulness (which slows to the
speed of experiencing life one moment at a time). While sensemaking
is natural, it is our capacity for thoughtful sensemaking that is the
differentiator in leadership. We learn to tolerate the frustration and
anxiety of not knowing (especially as we enter the "in-between" state).
The implications for leaders is that if our actions are preceded by a
true sensemaking and a willingness to not know, at least momentarily,
then meaningful change can occur.

We believe there is an important place for thoughtful sensemaking
in our leadership lives. The story of Peter gives us insight why:

*Peter was on the fast track. His energy and enthusiasm were unmatched.
Plus, Peter had the kind of work ethic that organizations love, arriving
early and staying late. As he moved up the ranks, his manager roles
were mostly operational in nature—a great match for his driven nature.
To reward his performance and broaden his leadership abilities, he was
eventually promoted into the director role for product planning. New
product development and introductions had stalled, and Peter was seen
as the motivational force needed to get things rolling again.*

Unfortunately, Peter's high energy "push" of stretch targets and his desire for rapid turnaround of the department never aligned to their true needs. He never fully understood the longer development cycles or the experimentation and the learning required. More importantly, he never developed the "open and collegial" relationships that are critical for shaping new ideas. The constant push for results put the team on the verge of burnout. Peter was moved back into an operations role, having never grasped the sensemaking and learning required in his new role.

Sensemaking is fundamentally the process of acting thoughtfully or bringing our thinking and acting into a back-and-forth relationship that promotes deeper understanding. It may be best explained by a story (made famous by Weick) about the little girl who, after being told to be sure of what she was thinking before she spoke, said:

"How can I know what I think 'til I see what I say?" [23]

The little girl was being told to think before she acted. She was revealing what we all know intuitively (but haven't fully recognized)—that you can act your way into understanding. She was revealing the essential truth about sensemaking:

Sensemaking is the process of making sense through thinking and act-ing–a process in which both are always at play.

Let's say we are puzzled by a situation. Like the little girl, we "act our way" to understanding by calling a colleague with more experience and asking:

Can I run something by you? I am having this challenge and think it might be related to this issue. Does that make sense?

In a world that is increasingly complex, confusing, and moving way too fast, we will have to learn to create these small learning cycles that help us learn as we go. Circles (symbolizing the pathway between

FROM and TO) represent a continuous cycle of learning as well as wholeness and harmony. We like the symbolism and the idea that a "circle" is the necessary response for our complex challenges where we have to learn our way forward.

Sensemaking allows us to move from anxiety to action—without getting ahead of ourselves. We don't get stuck over-planning, allowing us to quickly move ideas into tests. Each test, whether it be a failure or success, not only gives us a new real-world experience, it emboldens the next move. Small actions allow us to test our thinking in a way that promotes learning, giving us access to the next level of thinking. Here's a simple example of how it works:

> *You receive data that shows a higher defect rate than expected on a product line. You go to some of the frontline workers to see if they can help you make sense of the situation. They have a couple of ideas that seem plausible and can be quickly tested. You are excited about these early tests but also realize that you are just starting the sensemaking process.*

With this combination of thinking and acting (think of them as two sides of the same coin), we begin to learn our way to potential solutions. Again, the underlying principle is that we won't truly understand a situation until we take some action. No matter the size of the challenge, we still reflect and act our way to higher levels of meaning and understanding, keeping the cycles of learning small and manageable. With a deeper feel for the practice of thoughtful sensemaking, we are ready for the application of more structured learning initiatives.

Learning Initiatives

The idea of a learning initiative is to stimulate new "thinking and acting" by creating a learning challenge for the organization. These initiatives are often leader-led, providing direction to the overall change effort. In Jamie's broad discussions with the larger finance organization, the consensus was that the first learning initiative should be a "needs analysis" with their internal customers to get a renewed sense of priorities. The guiding question for this first learning initiative became: *What are the true needs of our internal customers?*

While a survey was designed to efficiently capture data from the various departments served, the finance liaisons who interfaced with the departments were given a true sensemaking challenge. They were asked to wade into an ongoing conversation with their internal clients to see what they could learn about their true needs.

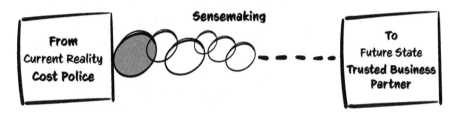

The shaded circle above represents the "needs analysis" being conducted by the larger organization. The smaller learning circles to the right of this initiative represent self-directed learning initiatives crafted by individuals and small teams as they try to "make sense" out of what it means to be a trusted business partner. These kind of "informal" actions are critical to effective sensemaking and were encouraged by the finance leadership team. For example, a finance liaison started running small tests with their facing department that were initiated through simple inquiries like the following:

What if we were able to conduct this kind of
sales analysis? Would that be helpful?

Referring to the earlier case study, we have updated our model below to show how sensemaking evolves from both planned and more spontaneous activities that will inspire new thinking, new conversations, and new actions.

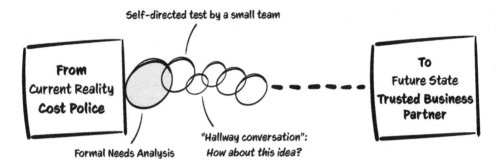

These small tests created "small wins" that were spontaneously shared across the organization, energizing the overall effort. The dashed line to the right of the learning circles symbolizes the ongoing and evolving nature of the transformation. Most importantly, the finance team was careful to not get ahead of themselves—not pretending to know what is next.

Shortly after this first initiative was underway, a second "department-wide" learning initiative was launched and is represented by the second shaded circle. The smaller circles to the right of this second shaded circle represent the more spontaneous learning that is stimulated by this larger, planned initiative. This second initiative was focused on understanding and developing the kinds of capabilities needed to become "trusted business partners." They quickly realized that this would be more than just adding new skills. They would be transitioning to a whole new identity within the organization. An initial study revealed a range of "theme areas" to be explored, including industry insight and knowledge, high-performance teaming, innovative analysis, collaborative consulting, and leadership.

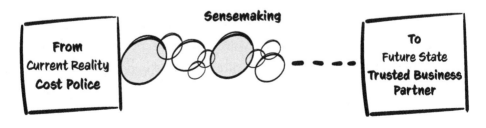

Let's pause and reflect on how our sensemaking path is evolving by contrasting it to the more linear and predictable path of a project (e.g., installing a software upgrade). In the case of a project, all of the steps can be envisioned at the start and a straightforward implementation schedule can be followed. In an overly simplified view, it would look like this (and we secretly wish that all of our change efforts would follow this path):

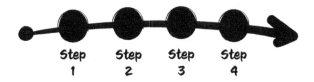

Step
1

Step
2

Step
3

Step
4

Sensemaking is about learning, and managing projects is more about implementation. Sensemaking evolves, often unpredictably. Projects can be carefully planned and efficiently executed. Sensemaking is a collective, meaning-making process. Managing projects follows well-defined routines. Hopefully, you can both see and feel the difference between the two.

The evolving, learning-centered, and unpredictable nature of sensemaking is captured in the circles of different size that appear in non-linear fashion. As shown earlier, some of the larger circles represent planned, leader-driven initiatives that stimulate the more spontaneous, smaller circles, which could represent a small experiment by a group or a stimulating conversation between two team members. While the larger initiatives bring some special focus to the change efforts, the smaller, self-directed efforts are critical to spreading the sensemaking and meaning-making efforts deep into the organization.

The sensemaking process also reveals how leaders need to be careful in exerting "control" over the process. If change efforts, big and small, need to pass though the hierarchy for approval, then we will lose access to the creative and naturally generated learning that is impossible to control or manage. However, the leader is also careful to provide the kind of direction and guidance that keeps the change activities focused. The leader-led initiatives or challenges can play this strategic role in shaping the arc of the journey without overly defining it.

The finance transformation reflected this pattern of high participation and empowered learning. However, for some of the finance team members, it was too much of a stretch. The new capabilities, like collaborative consulting, seemed disconnected from their analytical roles. As one finance employee put it ...

I feel like we were thrown into the deep end of
the pool after just one swim lesson.

For other team members, the new development opportunities created a sense of excitement and an opportunity to be more fully integrated into the business. One senior finance administrator described it this way:

I am definitely out of my comfort zone, but I am thinking about
the business in a whole new way. I was stuck in a mindset that
was focused too narrowly ... too much on the numbers.

A Final Reflection

While retaining the overall feel that we are on a transformational journey, the leader artfully balances between leading (being the "poet") and managing (being the "plumber"). As the poet, the leader shapes the early part of the journey with a new sense of possibility and experiments that challenge old ideas and practices. The "plumber" emerges as these new insights turn into new "plumbing projects" that add new "piping" to the current system. For example, a series of experiments imbedding finance professionals directly into the departments led to a "plumbing" project of implementing this strategy across the organization.

In just two years, the finance transformation had crossed an important threshold after successfully launching and supporting a range of initiatives. Conversation by conversation and small test by small test, they were fundamentally changing *what they did* and *who they were*. The transformation to being a "trusted business partner" was being recognized across the organization as being successful although certainly not complete. (In reality, our meaningful change journeys may never reach a final completion in the way that most of our projects do.) Realizing this, CFO Jamie crafted appropriate celebration moments that allowed the finance team to start claiming this new identity of "trusted business partner" without overstaying their time in the uncertainty of *betweenness.*

The new finance business cards eliminated official titles, replacing them with a single, common role:

Trusted Business Partner

Chapter Four
Self-Developing

The Art of Developing, Not Finding, Our True Self.

Not until we are lost do we begin to understand ourselves.
—Henry David Thoreau

Key Themes	Questions We Will Answer
The Timeless Question	*Who am I?*
Authentic Self-Developing	*Is there a true self?*
The Adaptive Self	*Is it OK to be less-than-true?*
The ME-WE Framing	*What does it mean to be both differentiated and integrated?*

We have come to our third and final practice in our meaningful change process, *self-developing*. We start with the question that philosophers, theologians, and psychologists have been struggling with for ages:

Who am I?

Is it the person I am today? Or is it the person I aspire to be? Is it best captured in my thoughts and feelings, or more truly rendered in my actions? All good questions, but as humans, we tend to believe that who we are is "fixed" to a large degree. This is one of our important pause points. It is not unusual for us to live under the notion that our true self is relatively fixed; otherwise, how could it be our true self? But these fixed views can be limiting to our ongoing growth.

Carol Dweck's game-changing research on the growth (vs. fixed) mindset offers insight.[24] According to Dweck, those who possess a fixed mindset are resistant to or fearful of change, averse to learning, and unwilling to self-evaluate or accept criticism. Dweck's research reveals that when people adopt a growth mindset, in contrast, they believe that their most basic abilities can be developed through dedication and hard work, with their intelligence and talents as only a starting point.[25] Dweck's work shows the power of our most basic beliefs about ourselves, which can either propel us forward or prevent us from fulfilling our potential. We believe this same philosophy can be applied to our concept of self-developing.

To this end, we need to cultivate a mindset toward continually growing a new (but truer) version of ourselves. Stephen, a new manager on a leadership team, is a great example.

Staying true to his introverted, private nature, Stephen has learned to share his ideas in smaller groups while developing high-trust relationships through his more natural one-on-one approach. With this foundation, he is pushing himself to take risks in larger group settings to feel part of the larger team.

It is also through the "self" that we ultimately shape the larger meanings in our life. Although it happens far too seldomly, the focus of any change initiative is essentially to redefine our identities, both organizationally and individually. It is our meaningful change initiatives that provide an opportunity for us rethink *who we want to become.* We also believe that ...

> *... our capacity for personal change is what makes our change initiatives possible.*

The idea of finding and expressing one's true self has also been a subject of interest in developing authentic leadership. Our approach focuses on character, with authentic self-development being simply

defined as: the degree we are being true to what we want to become
(not some fixed version of who we think we are). This task will not be
an easy one.

> *Much of who we are in organizational life is buried under the*
> *countless adaptations we make to meet the expectations of others.*

Here's the challenge: the better we know ourselves (our whole
selves), the more effectively we can interact with others. The more we
interact with others, the more we learn about ourselves. For example,
we might learn that we are biased against certain types of ideas, or we
may be surprised by our unexpected interest in exploring a new area.
In other words, interaction with others pulls us into the world in ways
we cannot do on our own. For this reason, we believe our authentic self grows best with and through others. We will show how the
"meaningful change" approach actually strengthens both our sense of
self-determination (our ME) and our need to belong and fully integrate
with others (our WE). As captured in our meaning framework below, it
is our authentic and growing identities that define the self-developing
process. What energizes this growth is the harmonizing of our ME
and WE.

Practice Area	Source of Meaning	Guiding Principle	Motivating Tension
Self-Developing	A growing identity	Authenticity	Self-determined vs. Belonging" (ME-WE)

Later in the chapter will return to our finance case study to show
how meaningful change can be a transformative experience for the
person. But to fully appreciate the authentic self, we need to better
understand our *adaptive self.*

The Adaptive Self

We were typically molded as children by our parents, teachers, clergy, friends, peers, and the larger culture to "fit in"—to be a true team player. As a result, we developed beliefs, thoughts, feelings, and behaviors that kept us acting in ways that weren't always developed from within. We learned to *adapt* to these external influences and pressures. In fact, this *ability to adapt* can be tied to our deepest survival instincts.[26] These survival instincts help us to tolerate difficult situations within our family, work, and other life situations. It is also the adaptive self that serves as a critical buffer in what can be a challenging and threatening world.

It can feel like the figure below, where the larger, most visible presence is the adaptive self that is negotiating our place in the world.

The adaptive self gives us time to do the necessary sensemaking before we fully reveal our true feelings. For example, when new to a job, the adaptive self helps us determine who we can trust, what are the boss's hot buttons, and where the potential land mines are hidden. Let's be clear, the first and foremost goal of the adaptive self is to protect us. Over time, as we learn the ropes and sense there is an adequate level of psychological safety in the work environment, we start to reveal more of our true self. This is only natural, with the act of self-disclosure sending a signal to others that we want to be more fully known.

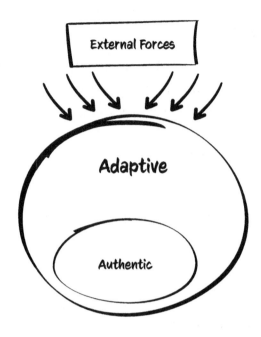

While the true self grows over time, the adaptive self remains necessary for navigating a challenging world. We are not "less than authentic" when we are adapting. For example, a colleague gets a coveted promotion that we were also being considered for. We are heartbroken but don't reveal our true feelings. We congratulate them and put our best face forward. A fellow colleague notes how well we are handling it. We confide in them that we are still working through it but want to be seen as a team player. That is understandable. Authenticity is not maintaining a strict coherence between what you feel and do. In fact …

… we can lose credibility when we disclose everything we feel.

As we adapt and grow, we will see our true self struggle with new and emerging identities. For example, Sam was recently promoted to a manager position and is adapting to the expectations and accountabilities of the new role. Initially, he felt the need to create some professional distance with those who once were peers. One-on-one communication actually felt awkward as he tried to maintain some kind of boss presence. With some coaching from a more experienced manager, Sam realized he was "role playing" and not only losing connection to his true self but losing credibility with his team.

Authenticity can be measured as the extent to which a person behaves in a way that feels personally self-determined. It feels more like a conscious choice than an automatic reaction. In other words, it is born out of the hard work of crafting a strong sense of character beyond one's personality traits. For example, a personality test reveals that Ellen is naturally competitive but lacks empathy. Deep down she knows this and accepts this finding but still feels the need to develop empathy as a character trait. In this way …

> *… authentic self-developing focuses more on being aware of one's desires for growth and is not limited to one's natural strengths.*

At some point on our development path, we will need to accept that we are imperfect beings in an imperfect world. Ironically, our lives can actually feel more meaningful by acknowledging what we are up against and not pretending things are OK. Our expectations for ourselves and others not only become more realistic, they become more empathic. We also begin to let go of the illusion that we can *always* do our best work or *always* be the best versions of ourselves. With this growing acceptance, we start to have different and more honest conversations with ourselves and others. More readily we admit our shortcomings, mistakes, and our need for help.

Here's where it gets interesting. Growing toward our true self is actually achieved through two different but complementary paths, the ME and the WE. As we shall see as we continue to examine the finance case study, our development along these two paths is both accelerated and deepened by our meaningful change initiatives. We start with an overview of the ME and WE development paths.

The ME-WE Framing

To get a deeper understanding of what it means to develop our true self, we present our ME-WE framing.[27] In essence, the ME (developing the authentic self) and the WE (developing our capacity to find meaning with and through others) represent the two necessary paths of our self-development efforts. The first path, the ME path, is inward and focuses on the personal side of leadership, where we discover the critical role that meaning plays in our own life. This may sound a bit strange but on the ME path …

… it's about you.

Of course, it is not about you in some ego-driven, self-centered way. Rather it is about the struggle in developing a sense of self as an autonomous and self-determined individual. If you do not make ongoing progress in this endeavor, you will be trapped in a life of conformity. The question we need to ask ourselves:

Are we living according to our own values and ethical principles, or are we automatically living according to the values and standards of other people?

The ME path is where we become uniquely different, viewing life with a curiosity, insightfulness, and thoughtfulness that can be transformative. By successfully differentiating and being true to our emerging self, we begin to positively influence others around us. Put simply, seeing someone act in an authentic, self-determined way is inspiring. For example, witnessing a colleague respectfully challenge the status quo with bold new thinking not only reveals their character but inspires us to do the same.

We also characterize the inner or ME journey as the path of developing our authentic leadership voice. In shaping this voice, we start to see what it truly means to act with integrity. It's not just the positive feelings that are generated when we do good things. It's the wholeness or completeness we feel when we act in alignment with the person we want to become. In terms of our psychological growth, we are becoming *differentiated*—increasingly self-determined, competent, and growing in authenticity.[28]

The second path of the journey, the outer WE path, is where we find our place in the world as we learn to serve beyond our own needs and we create new meaning with and through others. In terms of our social growth, we are becoming more fully *integrated* into the world, increasingly relational, collaborative, and service-oriented.[29] If we are successful, we begin to feel like a whole person, a person for the world. Unlike the ME path, the WE path is …

… not about you.

As we become more integrated with those around us, we start to understand the difference between learning alone and learning with others. Counterintuitively, learning with others (although messy) offers some significant advantages. For example, as individuals there are so many things we *almost know* and even more things we *almost do*. But the diversity and will of the larger group can pull us along in ways that we simply can't do on our own. We learn to "run at a different pace" that can move us beyond our own limiting and self-serving habits. As a more integrated person, we discover the paradox that by focusing on others, we amplify our own growth in a more natural way.

Over time, we learn the subtleties of this ME-WE dance as we move between inserting our voice and facilitating the voice of others. This is not an easy task, especially in light of our survival programming, which can make our own self-interests the default condition. In our case study company, Izzie is one of the more senior finance liaisons. You can see the tension in her reflection as she wrestles with a ME-WE dilemma.

"Initially I was more than just disappointed when the senior team went with John's recommendation over mine for framing the strategic learning initiative. I certainly was not in the mood to support the new direction. It took a day or two ... and some help from a friend ... but I started to see how John's proposal would serve us best over the long run. I know others could sense my disappointment and will be watching how I move forward. I have decided to bring an 'all in' attitude that leaves no doubt."

As we can see, resolving the natural tension between our ME and WE can take time, patience, and the kind of character that can see beyond our self-interest. This can be particularly hard to do in organizational life where individual achievement is often more valued than teamwork.

To visualize how the ME-WE dynamic works, we return to the simplicity of the Venn diagram. Below we show that there are actually three elements, with the WE being the intersection of ME and Others.

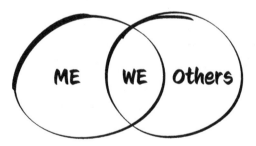

We learn to grow the *almond shape*, the WE area that represents the intersection of our shared interests. The WE area also represents our capacity to collaborate and work well together. In the finance case study, the ME is represented by members of the finance organization with "others" represented by the departments they are serving. The

WE represents their collaborative efforts with the representatives from their facing departments.

As one of their development exercises, the leaders in the finance organization asked each team member to visually capture the current size of the almond (or level of WE-ness). Not surprisingly, at the start of the change journey, most team members showed only a small intersection in their picture (as shown below). This simple but intuitive exercise always reveals in stark visual clarity what cannot be expressed in words alone.

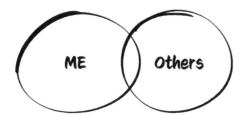

The leaders then asked: *How might we grow the almond?* Dozens and dozens of responses led to the types of conversations and actions that would build stronger relationships. For example, it was this exercise where the "embed in the department" idea was shared:

> *"We need to co-locate in the departments we serve. We will never be fully accepted until we do."*

The next question the leaders asked brought a personal accountability and a special energy to growing the ME-WE overlap. The leadership team asked:

> *"What can you personally bring to enhance the larger change effort?"*

This question not only taps into their ME-ness or natural strengths but also helps them to see how they can serve others with their talents. The responses, like these below, always help to create a special sense of WE-ness for a group.

"I am good at organizing things. I will help keep us on track."
"I can ensure our meetings are focused and productive."
"You can count on me to say what needs to be said."

Over the two-year change period, the finance department team members participated deeply in the sensemaking efforts as they not only helped to frame the learning initiatives but played the primary roles in running the small learning experiments that brought them to life. One of the breakthroughs started as a hallway conversation between two finance team members. One had an insight on how they could more reliably predict market demand over the short term. The idea got teased out into an application that allowed both sales and marketing to focus their monthly plans more tightly.

To play these larger roles required ongoing development in terms of understanding the business more fully and developing the kinds of broad collaborative and consultative skills that could earn the moniker of "trusted business partner." However, not all of the finance team made the journey. Some became frustrated by the "need to continuously adapt" to the shifting requirements of the change process and the new role demands that took them out of their comfort zones. Others, however, were transformed by the journey as they grew both their ME and WE capabilities in ways that would not have been accessible in their regular jobs.

In terms of ME growth, their ongoing sensemaking efforts help to cultivate a new sense of self that is best captured by the statement from Les, one of the finance representatives:

"I felt like I was always testing my limits. There were days where I really wanted to leave the organization. But it was worth the struggle. I have a newfound confidence in myself and my ability to contribute to the business."

Their WE capabilities also grew dramatically as their collaboration and teaming skills were shaped over the two years. As finance team member Beth put it:

"It took some time before I felt comfortable with the messy collaboration challenges we committed to. I learned to adapt ... to fake it until I could make it. More and more I feel like I truly belong to this organization."

Our review of the three practice areas is now complete, and we can finalize our model to reflect all of the elements. The "learning circles" that represent the sensemaking path also represent the path of self-discovery. As we noted before, *what we do* and *who we are* become almost inseparable when we seek meaningful change. The logic is simple:

> *As we shift what we do, it begins to change who we are.*
> *As we change who we are, it begins to shift what we do.*

In the case of our finance employees, as they started to do things more aligned with "trusted business partner," a new identity began to take shape. As this new identity grew, they would naturally engage in these supporting actions with less conscious effort. They were beginning to embody their new purpose, symbolically represented in a common path of sensemaking and self-developing. Plus, the circle best represents the cyclical and non-linear nature of all personal development.

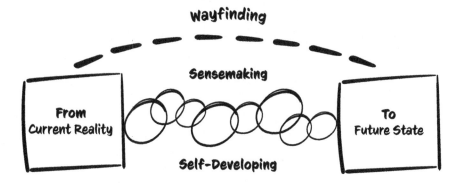

A Final Reflection

As expected, none of this meaningful change stuff works without the kind of "purposeful leadership" that actively models and supports both a strong ME and WE. It is our experience that it is the lack of leadership that contributes most to the 70% change failure rate. Below is a simple framework we have used to help leaders prepare for their challenging transformation roles.

To get the attention of leaders, we create four possible personas by charting whether leaders are high or low in their ME and WE.

	High WE	High WE	
Low ME	*Loyal Follower*	*Purposeful Leader*	High ME
Low ME	*MIA*	*High Achiever*	High ME
	Low WE	Low WE	

The four resulting personas are:

High Achiever: Driven to get results through a big ME, they often enjoy great career success. However, they lack integration (WE-ness) with others and have difficulty serving beyond their individual agenda.

MIA (Missing In Action): Lacking both ME and WE growth, they provide limited value beyond their basic job duties.

Loyal Follower: Their low ME and high WE are revealed in their overly compliant and passive behavior.

Purposeful Leader: Their high ME and WE creates a purposeful and collaborative style that earns the leader designation, irrespective of their job title. It is the "purposeful leader" who is best equipped to create meaningful change.

Our experience with this framing reveals that too much ME, the *high achiever* persona, can thwart the sense of shared purpose and commitment in a team. On the flip side, too much WE can promote passivity and conformity, creating too many *loyal followers*. In our leadership development work over the last decade, our participants readily admit to finding themselves in these two quadrants too often. The finance managers made this admission as well. It is understandable given that organizational life can promote both of these conflicting styles: high personal achievement to advance your career while at the same time conforming to the wishes of those above you.

The good news is that this framework is intuitive in nature. It doesn't take a lot of explanation. Once a leader understands the different dimensions, they can start to align their actions more fully in the *purposeful leadership* quadrant. As one senior manager revealed:

> *I keep the ME-WE framework on my desk. It serves as a reminder that I carry into my conversations and meetings throughout the day. I have gotten much better at recognizing when it's "about me" and when it's "not about me." I also find myself reflecting more and asking myself tough questions like ...*

> *Do I need to more fully involve my colleagues on this issue?*
> *Do I need to take a stronger stand with my boss?*
> *How will this decision be perceived by others?*

In the next chapter, we leverage the principle of *everydayness* as both a key strategy for integrating our meaningful change efforts fully into each day and as a way to continually grow the self.

Chapter Five
Everydayness

Instead of Busyness

How we spend our days, of course, is how we spend our lives.
—Annie Dillard

Key Themes	Questions We Will Answer
Everydayness	*Why is "everydayness" essential to creating meaningful change?*
Intention Setting	*How do intentions lead us to deeper levels of meaning and expression?*
Meaningful Conversations	*How did we lose connection to our capacity to converse and how do we regain it?*
Minding the Moments, Telling Our Stories	*How do "moments" help us to rethink our orientation to time?*

Everydayness

We love this word. By adding "ness" to everyday, it communicates the "quality of being everyday." We live our lives in days, and what we do daily has the best chance of becoming part of *who we are.* We also affirm that …

Nothing changes until we do.

When we do change, a sense of purpose and engagement ensues that can be transformative. However, if our personal development efforts sit at the edge of our days, they will be replaced by a *busyness* that can be numbing.

In reclaiming our days, we learn to leverage the power of *everydayness* to bring our meaningful change initiative fully into our day—not letting it take a back seat to the typical urgencies that always ensue. *Everydayness* also brings the necessary rhythm and regularity to the personal self-development we seek as leaders. To achieve these ends, we have aligned an *everydayness* strategy with each of our three practices.

Practice Area	*Source of Meaning*	*Everydayness Strategy*
Wayfinding	A purposeful direction	Setting intentions
Sensemaking	A sense of knowing	Meaningful conversation
Self-Developing	A growing identity	Minding the moments and telling our stories

This is also one of those times where we wish we could be sitting across from you at a coffee shop, engaging in a heartfelt discussion on why these three everydayness strategies are game changers. Just reading about them may not reveal their true and transforming nature. They may feel "too familiar" or even feel like things you are already doing. We will try to convince you otherwise.

Most importantly, these three elements feed off of each other and are hard to separate as they come together as a powerful meaning-making practice. Practices, by their nature, are process-driven and require a mindfulness, discipline, and attention not typically experienced in our daily routines. We start the exploration of everydayness with intention setting.

Intention setting

Beyond the necessary goal setting and planning that accompanies all change, we have found that there is one practice that is essential to wayfinding:

Intention setting

To fully grasp the power of intentions, we start with a story:

Our friend Anne likes to ride her bike on the beach and will often set a goal of riding anywhere from six to ten miles. It takes a bit of a commitment to load the bike and drive 30-plus minutes to the beach. One time, after meeting her ten-mile goal, Anne realized that during the ride, her thoughts were consumed with a work-related problem that was getting the best of her. As she loaded her bike back into the car, she realized that she'd barely noticed the wonderful surroundings of the beach during her ride. She could have ridden her bike in her neighborhood! Plus, she lost the opportunity to get some needed distance (and inspiration) from the problem she was working through.

Now, she sets a new intention prior to taking her first pedal at these beach trips. Sitting comfortably on the saddle, she quietly reviews her intention to leave her problems in the car and to fully experience the beauty that makes these rides so special. She also commits to pausing at times along the route, taking a break from the purposeful pedaling and just breathing as she takes in the world around her. She also gives herself permission to daydream, noodling and giving life to some of her new aspirations. Amazingly (but not surprisingly), Anne reveals that this new intentionality "shrinks" the problems she left waiting in the car.

Anne always reaches her mileage goal. Her intentions shape "how" she reaches this outcome. We can see how goals and intentions shape different kinds of behaviors. Goals focus on future outcomes. Intentions, on the other hand, focus us on the present, bringing a special energy to the moments right in front of us. This is especially critical for building momentum in our meaningful change initiatives. Our change initiatives evolve over time and don't have the predictable pacing of a project. Without daily intentions, our change efforts will lose ground to the always-present urgencies of the day.

So how do we do it? As we noted, a practice is a process, and we have learned that there are three steps in effective intention setting.

One: Set the tone
Two: "Sit with" the change
Three: Set specific intentions

One: Set the Tone

Let's be clear, the practice of intention setting, as part of the overall "everydayness" strategy, must be done before the day "officially" begins (which also could be the night before). Our experience shows that the typical intention-setting session by a leader will range from 10 minutes to 30 minutes, an incredible ROI for the time and energy invested. It starts with creating the necessary time and space, which is not only protected but creates a special sense of presence as we lean into *what's possible?*

In an open, reflective spirit, we sit safely on the balcony of our life and spend a few moments in gratitude. We have reached another one of our special pause points. This expression of gratitude may feel like one of those optional "feel good" steps. Actually, it is way more.

This step, more than anything else we have experienced, has the potential to transform us and the quality of our days. While we tend to think of gratitude as a feeling, research continues to demonstrate its value as a *practice*, as we learn to appreciate what surrounds us.[30] When we do so, all kinds of benefits accrue, starting with our physical and mental health and extending to our relationships, resilience, and self-esteem.[31] In short, when we practice gratitude, both our ME (our internal resources) and our WE (our connections to the external world) not only grow, they thrive.

Gratitude starts with a simple appreciation for the goodness in life—our family, friends, and the little dog sitting on our lap. We can see them in our minds or whisper their names under our breath. We then shift to our upcoming day, as this sense of gratitude opens us up to the larger opportunities that await. It's like the author with a great idea for a story and a blank page in front of her. As poet David Whyte reminds us:

> *... there is a small opening into the new day*
> *which closes the moment you begin your plans.*
> *What you can plan is too small for you to live.*

We also start to envision our meaningful change effort. We want to put it at the center of our day. We "practice" appreciating both the opportunities and challenges that will undoubtedly come our way. We are even thankful for the struggles, knowing how they have stretched us in new directions. This "pre-work" creates a frame of mind that will serve us later in the day when things do not go as planned. Amazingly, we can find meaning, grace, and gratitude in our low points and the inevitable shortfalls.

Two: "Sit With" the Change

We have set the tone and now it is time to "sit with" our change. We start by envisioning the meaningful change we have committed to. It is often helpful to have our supporting documents for the initiative close at hand to help us visualize how the FROM-TO journey is coming to life. As we sit with our initiative, we sense the imbalances. Maybe we are stuck in "discovery mode" and have too many balls in the air. Or we could be short-changing the learning process and moving too quickly into implementation with half-baked ideas. As we sit above the fray, simple wayfinding questions naturally emerge:

> *Is the team fully engaged around the new direction?*
> *What elements need special support at this time?*
> *What special recognitions or appreciations are due?*

We sit with these questions, letting both our head and heart do their work. With this overview accomplished, we are ready to set specific intentions.

Three: Set Specific Intentions

With both a sense of gratitude and an intuitive feel for what is needed for our change initiative, we set our specific intentions for the day. For example, after sitting with the change, there may be signs that parts of the organization are lagging in their support for the initiative. Exploratory conversations with these groups will now become priorities for the day. We know this can't be handled in the hallway or through e-mail. We are committed to making the time to fully understand what is going on and make the necessary progress. Many leaders also find it helpful to commit their intentions to writing. This visual documentation further imprints our intentions. We are leveraging the power of the list: *What gets written, gets done.*

CFO Jamie, from our finance case study, provides an illustrative example of how to do it.

We see Jamie still at home, sitting at her kitchen table with a second cup of coffee. It just takes a few moments, but her gratitude exercise centers her. For six months now, Jamie has been setting her daily intentions, and it now feels like an essential ritual that she rarely misses. This time to ruminate creates an emotional connection to her intentions and allows them to grow in new ways.

With a few key documents and her notebook in front of her, she begins to gain some perspective on how their journey to "trusted business partner" is progressing. Overall she is feeling good about the progress and is starting to noodle the idea of a milestone celebration to allow for some timely recognition of what has been accomplished, including appreciation for the extra work that has been taken on by the larger organization. She plans to share the idea with her leadership team today.

Jamie is also sensing that a key initiative is getting bogged down due to its new technology requirements. She has a strong relationship with the CIO and knows she will bring some good news to the team on these stalled efforts. She checks the CIO's calendar and sends a meeting request. She also carves out time for a special training initiative she is leading. Her intent is to make enough progress today to be able to announce it to the organization.

Like the rest of us, Jamie also knows what it means to get bogged down and distracted by the urgencies of an impending day. She feels empowered by her intention setting, which brings a sense of control to what can be an unwieldy day. Jamie has also learned to integrate her intention-setting practice throughout the day. As she is heading to an important meeting, she naturally begins to muse …

… what is it that I truly want to accomplish in this session?

We can start to see how our intentions are often evidenced through the conversations we have throughout the day, and we will see how intentions play a special role in making conversations effective.

Meaningful Conversation

Face-to-face conversation is central to our lives, but in many respects it has lost its relevance as technology has become the dominant medium that connects us. But an e-mail, text, or post simply can't replace the meaning-making capabilities of a conversation. In fact, it is through conversation that we enhance our sensemaking, shape our possibilities, and form the relationships that will make meaningful change possible. But here's the question:

Why are real conversations uncommon in our organizational lives?

Part of the challenge is that we simply don't like to slow to the speed of conversation. It takes more time, more psychic energy, and more skill than an e-mail or text. It can wear you out. Plus, the urgent nature of many of our work demands has dramatically downshifted our expectations for conversing. Too often our conversations feel one-way, transactional, and overly efficient. As a result, when true innovation and collaboration are needed, we often lack the patience and skills to engage at a more thoughtful and sensemaking pace.

Clearly, there is a need for deeper dialogue and sensemaking in the workplace. Our special focus relates to conversations where sensemaking is needed to deal with these challenges. It not only requires that we recommit to a more meaningful form of conversation in our work lives, but also that we invest in the kind of personal capabilities that make conversations work.

In shaping the conversation, we intentionally seek to create synergy between those who have a stake in the change process.

The image we want to create is not a back-and-forth exchange (I talk and then you get to talk) but the *flow of meaning* between participants. We have all probably experienced those special conversations that have created deeper understanding of an issue and have deepened our relationships as well.

Nothing quite bonds like the meeting of minds.

> *The notion that our lives succeed or fail on conversations one at a time is at once commonsensical and revolutionary.*
>
> – Ken Blanchard

Conversations are the core process through which individuals think together and organizations learn. As we saw in the finance case, it is through conversation that we create new shared meanings while deepening our relationships. The back-and-forth between thinking and testing new ideas continues until someone says:

"I think we have a great idea emerging. Let's test it!"

It is through conversation that we make sense of our shared experience, explore possibilities, test our assumptions, and create the supporting rationale for our next actions. In other words, *we learn.* As a practice, meaningful conversations are best served as a mindful process of *clarifying intentions* and *learning together.* Let's briefly explore each element.

Clarifying intentions. Let's face it. Conversations are challenging and can easily lose their way. Leveraging our new insights around intentionality, it is best to start by clarifying intentions. This will establish a sense of purpose and focus for the discussion. The finance team members found it productive to not only clarify intentions but to structure some of the questions or discussion topics in advance to keep the conversation productive and flowing. For example, one team member said, *"I'd like to better understand how our market analysis can better meet your needs. I've prepared a few questions to get the ball rolling. Does that sound like a good place to start?"* The team member, in a very simple way, confirmed the topic and the desired outcome and also identified the process (asking prepared questions). That is "intention setting" at its best.

Learning together. Conversations can lose their synergy (and potential to further develop the relationship) when we try to get someone to adopt our way of seeing things. Of course, we want to influence others with our ideas and to differentiate ourselves, but too many conversations in organizational life are stymied by the desire to impose our viewpoint. But here is the problem. No matter how articulate and logical we may be, we won't capture the engagement and support of others without involving them deeply in the process. The best way to do this is by keeping the conversation in a "learning mode," where new ideas are tested and debated openly. The "what if" question best captures this learning intention:

What if we tried this?

We now come to our third and final everyday practice, one that can support both intention setting and meaningful conversation practices.

Minding the Moments ... and Telling Our Stories

Minding the moments, as a personal practice, reveals how the "quality of our attention" may be the most differentiating element in living out our lives at work. It is not about trying to live each moment to the fullest. That would be exhausting!

For the most part, we act as if there is simply not enough time, leading us to do lots of dumb things as we feel the pressure to act throughout the day. But what makes the "minding the moments" framing so special is that it allows us to rethink and renegotiate our sense of time. A moment is an actual unit of time: three seconds, according to some researchers.[32] That's because three seconds is the minimal time it takes us to experience something.

For example, it may take about three seconds to realize that you are feeling tired. Or that the grumbling in your stomach means you are hungry. And that flash of brilliance you get in the shower? It takes about three seconds to grasp this idea before you can quickly exit the shower and write it down!

So, if a moment is three seconds, how many moments are there in a day? Well, after subtracting eight hours for sleeping, the remaining sixteen hours translate into 20,000 waking moments every day. Let that sink in. When every new day rolls around, we have 20,000 new moments to utilize. We also know that it takes just a few moments to make someone's day, whether with a compliment or a shared laugh.

So, our first realization is that we have plenty of time, even though we act as if we don't (rushing through things and potentially missing the uniqueness hidden in some of our moments). Our *minding the moments* practice is about cultivating the kind of presence that moves us beyond the "busyness" that captures way too much of our days. It's not about managing time better, but rather it is a practice that seeks balance between …

Doing and Being

> *We have never arrived. We are in a constant state of becoming.*
> –Bob Dylan

Many leaders in organizations feel they are living (sometimes exclusively) on the "doing" side of this pair, trapped in a world of activity, production, and adaptation. We believe that through *minding the moments*, we can be open to fully experience "moments of truth" that can blow by us undetected. We experience a "transient and unfulfilling" sense of self when we get lost in our busyness. Loren, in a manager role for the finance organization, describes the challenge this way:

"Before our change effort, I didn't know how to slow down. There was always some urgent challenge that would consume me. When we learned about our ME and WE, it really hit me. I realized I was always on—with no neutral gear—eating my lunch (typically a Power Bar) while I processed e-mails. My sense of self, my ME, was hopelessly lost in activities, many of them meaningless. My connections to others, my WE, was transactional at best. That is also changing as we seek to not only develop ourselves but to serve others."

It is only when we can bring both a self-awareness and a mindful presence to our ME and WE efforts that it will be possible to lead the change we seek. It all starts with the simple pause. It takes just a moment:

one thousand one ... one thousand two ...
one thousand three

Take one more moment for a deep breath. Maybe just one more. In just a few moments we start to feel a sense of calmness replace our amped-up physiology.

Consider the difference between "fast thinking" and "slow thinking." According to Daniel Kahneman, our fast system for thinking is overconfident, rapid, and generates ideas hastily.[33] It certainly has its advantages in our complex world that values action. However, in complex situations, fast thinking limits our broader review beyond known options and fixed patterns of response—often leading us down the wrong path.

The slow thinking system, according to Kahneman, is more deliberate and logical—able to undertake deeper thought processing.[34] This system is more appropriate for executing our practices. It is also through our slow thinking that we develop personal capabilities best, dramatically expanding our range of responses. So, how do we choose? Go with the fast and instinctive self or the more deliberate and rational one?

Pause and ...

It all starts with the pause. The pause creates that necessary break between stimulus (a problem appears) and response (we take action). When we pause, we get the opportunity to choose. In just a moment or two, we can start to discern that what we are about to do has real consequences. We feel the pressure to move forward, but pausing— just for a moment—gives us just enough mindful presence to keep our instinctive reactions in check.

Not only does pausing help to relax and center us (giving our nervous system a needed break), pausing gives us options. Our boss asks us a question. Instinctively, we want to show that we are knowledgeable. In the past, we may have "faked" an answer, but we all know how that goes. Our more authentic self … pauses … realizes that they don't have the answer … and responds more appropriately … buying time … "*I will have that answer for you right away.*"

You have probably also noticed that you operate best when you alternate between periods of focus and periods of renewal. We can only do so much writing before we need a break. When we come back, we feel refreshed and energized, with new energy and insights. Without the break or brief renewal, we would be pushing a rock up the hill. In fact, very few people can work intensely for periods beyond an hour without a break. So, we pause.

How long should we pause? Well, it depends on the situation. The more emotional the issue, the longer the pause. The more complex the issue, the longer the pause. The more sensemaking that is needed, the longer the pause. In fact, a walk around the block may be needed to get some necessary distance from the issue. We also know that a good night's sleep will not only enhance our perspective but will often cut a problem in half!

For our everydayness approach, it is the little pauses throughout the day that become the focus of our *minding the moments* practice. Here's the cool thing: we always get a little warning when it is time to pause. We feel it in our body. Imagine a colleague delivers a cutting remark about your proposal in a meeting. You feel your face flush, your sense of presence is shaken, and anger starts to creep in. So …

… you pause.

As you can see, pausing is being. It not only seeks to create a neutralizing space between stimulus and response, it also serves as a launch point for a range of strategies that bring out the best in ourselves—and others.

Pause and breathe.
Pause and sip some tea.
Pause and reframe the situation.
Pause and walk around the block.
Pause and just observe what is going on.
Or when things get really tough ... pause and call your mom.

Behind each one of these simple and intuitive strategies are opportunities for new practices to shape our everydayness. For example, when problems or challenges get complex, we sometimes artificially reduce the complexity by acting like we know more than we do. While that can be temporarily reassuring, it will not unleash our deeper resources. A much better strategy is to pause and ask questions. It relieves us of the burden of "not knowing" and creates a powerful learning pathway for both us and others.

Questions not only help us to think things through in a safe way, they can help to build rapport and trust among team members. Questions also tend to enhance the emotional intelligence in the room as we become more aware of how others (including ourselves) feel and think about an issue. Another simple but profound practice is to pause and observe. The intent is not to judge your experience but to observe it. For example, we try not to label our emotions as good or bad, they just are.

As we learn to take an observer's view, instead of being overwhelmed by an emotion, our detachment allows us to take a more curious view as to why we feel a certain way. Obviously, this takes work and discipline, as most of us are conditioned to let our emotions take over in the heat of the moment. But once we have seen the calming effect on our nervous system, we are motivated to cultivate this practice further. The pause points to the deeper capacity that is getting tons of attention today—the deeper sense of being and knowing that come through being more mindful. With a new sense of pacing in our lives, we can learn to pause and ...

... tell our story.

Telling our individual or collective stories is critical to the change process. It often starts with the overarching story of the larger organization—its foundational narrative—which reveals its passion, purpose, and mission. We see organizations go to great lengths to keep this story alive. But equally important, it is through story that we create and attach meaning to our individual and team change efforts. Without a sense of "why" we are pursuing a change, the challenge of leading true change will inevitably stall. We may manage the change to some kind of limited "face-saving" victory, but there will be no transformation of what we do or who we are.

We connect storytelling to our moments metaphor because it is often through our capacity to pause and manage the moments that a story can evolve. For example, we have all experienced those moments of truth where our story comes alive. Imagine a handful of us are sitting together in a conference room on a Friday evening. It is way past the normal quitting time, but we are at a critical decision point. We believe our project is well conceived and has potential, but unanticipated challenges and barriers keep emerging. More than frustrating, the lack of progress is negatively impacting team dynamics.

This emergency meeting is to decide whether we continue or cut our losses. The conversation that follows is decidedly emotional. But each voice seems to embolden the next voice. Although we are at the end of the week, at the low point of our emotional capacities, we find a resolve and a consensus to continue. As we leave the room, we feel a special sense of unity and purpose with each other.

After that evening, that story, *the Friday night story*, is told over and over again in both our conscious and unconscious minds. Just being together now reminds us of what happened. We are seeing each other differently. But more importantly, it becomes part of our collective narrative, the ongoing capture of our change efforts. Although we provide the rational, form-driven weekly updates on our change progress, it in no way captures what happened on Friday evening. The grit, pluck, and resilience that energized that meeting is also shaping the deepest, most authentic parts of who we are. *You can't get that through filling out a standard form.*

We can start to see how these moments of truth will not only become part of our unifying story, they will lead us into a deeper questioning of why our change efforts matter. They also inspire each of us to make sense and find meaning in our own personal stories. This is not always an easy task. Meanings are fragile and so are our identities in a change-riddled world. Consider Ingrid's emerging story.

Lately, Ingrid has been ending her day on the phone with her best friend, Ellen. Things have been challenging at work, as a reorganization will transfer a good portion of her current role to another department. The move makes sense from a business perspective but has undermined her sense of identity. Until now, Ingrid's story was one of being the "go to" person on the team, and her reduced role has shattered that.

She confides in Ellen, "I keep telling myself scary stories. Is this the end of me?" Artfully, Ellen shifts the conversation to the possibilities of growing her current role and establishing a new sense of self. After a couple of what Ellen characterizes as "tough love" sessions, Ingrid starts to reimagine her story of loss as a story of opportunity. The small steps she is now taking to expand her role renew her sense of purpose. Seeing a new truth, Ingrid reveals to Ellen:

"That reorganization may have been a blessing in disguise."

As we all have undoubtedly experienced, even a rational business decision can disrupt the patterns of meaning across individuals and teams. As with the case of Ingrid, we need others to hear our stories and help us to reshape them. Through the reimagining of our story, we get to restore the sense of meaning to the larger arc we call our life. Failing to do so leaves us anxious and vulnerable, less than whole. Leadership is not only about creating meaningful change but also about attending to the meaning that can come from it.

Let's face it. Organizational life, with its inevitable failures and setbacks, becomes livable through meaning-making. The failed deal gets reframed into a new opportunity. The long hours and sacrifices are now paying off with an unexpected breakthrough. The range of emotions and personal growth that come with these change journeys reshape us, become part of our character and identity. When the next change challenge emerges, we don't just bring our newfound resilience, we bring our continuing story with us. We get to say things like …

"That was the toughest year of my life but look where I am now. I can't wait to tell you my story."

Creating meaningful change is reflected most clearly in the stories that emerge. By telling the story, we make sense out of the change—especially the parts that brought us to our knees. As noted earlier, Joseph Campbell's work on the "hero's journey" reveals how the most enduring stories are those in which a character struggles mightily but eventually prevails. The plumber in us wants to get back to work, but the poet in us knows that we will have to facilitate and make time for the stories that need to emerge at both the individual and group level. The most powerful request that facilitates meaningful change is simply:

Tell me your story.

> *Poetry is often the art of overhearing yourself say things you didn't know you knew. It is a learned skill to force yourself to articulate your life, your present world or your possibilities for the future.*
>
> –David Whyte

A Final Reflection

We live in an age of increasing anxiety and doubt as we struggle to create a strong sense of self that will measure up to the demands of the world.[35] It is certainly not surprising that mindfulness has moved into the mainstream, and research continues to validate the link between our sense of well-being and our ability to be present.[36]

We believe the capacity to create meaningful change is sustained by our ability to *be* … and to be in the moment. It is in this small safe harbor that sensemaking, truth-telling, reflection, and renewal can be exercised daily so that we can weather the storms that rage as we transition into the unknown. Our willingness to manage these moments ultimately rewards us with a sense of clarity and focus that cannot be restrained.

Instead of responding at the speed of thought, we move at the speed of thoughtfulness:

one thousand one … one thousand two … one thousand three…

Final Thoughts for the Journey Forward

First, thank you for taking the journey with us. We hope it has been a rewarding one. As you have witnessed, our *creating meaningful change* approach begins with the consistency and constancy of character. It also brings clarity to our complementary leading-managing roles as both poet (I create meaning) and plumber (I make things flow). Both are needed and valued in the change process.

As expected, not all of the change efforts we have helped to facilitate have reached their "TO" state. In fact, most had to endure multiple setbacks and failures along the way. But nothing grabs our attention like failure. It's how we respond to failure that may be the most developmental aspect of leading change. In our sensemaking practice, we learn to embrace failure by "failing fast and small." Our focus is on capturing the learning without losing momentum. We cultivate an attitude best captured in the Thomas Edison quote:

"I have not failed. I've just found 10,000 ways that won't work."

The length (fifteen years) and depth (over 1,000 participants) of this leadership development process has not only provided ongoing refinements but has enabled us to grow the meaningful change process in new ways. However, it has always been grounded in the simple question:

What is the meaningful change we seek?

Our map is now complete. As it has done for others, we hope it illuminates the path for creating meaningful change in your organizational life. It is through *wayfinding* that the leader naturally grows outward—while growing their team's purpose and identity in compelling new ways. We learn to hold the tension of *betweenness*, leaving the comfort of our current knowledge to explore new truths and cross new thresholds. This part of the journey brings great satisfaction as we see clearly how we and our organization can bring good into the world.

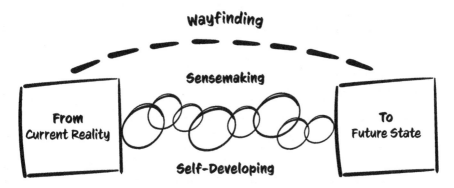

We also learn how finding our way, in a world that is increasingly complex and unknown, will require a deeper *sensemaking* than we have previously known. Too much of our work lives is characterized as "almost." We almost understand things. Almost gets us close but is simply not enough. We counter this condition by infusing our sensemaking efforts with thoughtfulness. It is thoughtful sensemaking that balances thinking and action in a way that promotes the kind of ongoing learning needed to transcend the equivocal nature of our work lives. Over-planning and overly conceptual strategies will have to give way to a new pragmatism best captured in the statement:

Let's start now ... with this small step.

As we also learned, we never find our true self, but get to spend a lifetime in self-discovery. Meaningful change efforts are what stimulate the most growth, positively shaping new capabilities. Along the way, the increasing stability and authenticity of our identities compel us to move through life's challenges with passion and purpose. We know who we are—and who we want to be. We also learn to bring a spirit of *everydayness* to our self-development, with the day being the perfect container to capture the incremental nature of personal growth.

We also hope you have found meaning to be the stabilizing rudder that is needed in this constant sea of change. The creation of meaning does this by cutting through the complexity of organizational life and highlighting what is most important. The pursuit of meaning, however, is a never-ending conversation we have with ourselves and others over a lifetime. The clarity reflected in these conversations will be critical to creating meaningful change.

As we are able to make small steps toward finding and developing our meanings, we are rewarded with a deep sense of participation that can overcome the powerlessness we often face in our organizational lives. As in any journey, each step we take brings a sense of anticipation, renewal, and fulfillment.

In our introduction, we showed how our meaningful change framework compares to other change models, hoping to reveal why ours is needed now more than ever. We hope that our "change framing" has met the promise of bringing us back home to the simplicity of Lewin's three-phase approach while capturing the essence of what it means to be fully human in our work lives. We also hope you can advance this model with your own experiences and insights, with plenty of opportunities to continue the discussion on our website. We can't wait to hear your voice.

Lewin	Cooperrider & Srivastava	Beer, Eisenstat & Spector	Kotter	Morrison & Kofford
3 phases	4 phases	6 steps	8 steps	3 practices
Unfreeze Transition Refreeze	Discovery Dream Design Destiny	Mobilizing Shared Vision Build Consensus Spread To All Monitor/Adjust Institutionalize	Sense of Urgency Guiding Coalition Create a Vision Communicate It Empower Others Short-Term Wins Consolidate Institutionalize	Wayfinding Sensemaking Self-Developing

Lastly, we note that our organizational lives are filled with choice. We believe those choices can be enhanced by simply asking: *What is the meaningful change we seek?* Faithfully answering this question will always connect us to something larger than ourselves, something that will unify us.

Depending on our spiritual foundations, meaning will play some role in the larger questions with which we will grapple.

Am I on the right path?
Am I making a difference?
Are my relationships sound and growing?

But let's pause and appreciate—truly appreciate—that if questions like these are the ones we face, then we are truly blessed.

We will see you on the journey,

Mike and Clint

Appendix One

Examples of Wayfinding Journeys

	FROM	TO
Consumer Products Division *Heat from the parent company*	*Buying the Market*	*Customer-Centered Growth*
Hospital Unit *Somebody help!*	*Lone Rangers*	*Happy to Help*
College Prep School *The purposeful school*	*College Admissions Madness*	*Developing Leaders for a New World*
Community Counseling Services *Let's think about this*	*Isolated on Zoom*	*Best of Both Worlds*

Change as Story

Outlined above are four case studies illustrating different FROM-TO journeys. These additional cases will not only enhance your understanding of the *wayfinding* practice but also reveal the range of diverse application opportunities. More than representative "business" cases, they also tell a story that reveals the potential of meaningful change efforts.

Some of these FROM-TO journeys were highly focused on transforming a single behavior while others sought to transform an organization. Also, a range of organizations are represented (e.g., profit, nonprofit, consumer products, health related, school systems, etc.) to show the adaptability of the change method. Framing the FROM-TO journey and crossing the threshold into "betweenness" is how the way-finding comes to life. It sets up the sensemaking and self-discovery practices that allow us to reimagine *what we do* and *who we are*.

Most importantly, these cases tell a "human-centered" story, creating an emotional attachment that information or data alone can't achieve. That's why we openly share the failures and emotional elements that often get left out of how we communicate in our work lives. Frequently, we "Photoshop" the blemishes and scars that give us a truer picture of what actually occurred. However, there is nothing more compelling than a story that reveals courage in the face of the failure and ongoing uncertainty that characterize any kind of meaningful change.

Finally, we hope you can also see how these narratives become part of the group's shared experience, connecting them in ways not achievable through the routine of their daily work. In every case, these stories "lived on" and continued to strengthen both individual and group identities while facilitating a special resilience as new challenges were faced together.

Scalable to Your Meaningful Change

It is also important to note that our FROM-TO journeys can scale to any situation requiring meaningful change. We will provide a brief overview of four other diverse wayfinding examples where leaders within organizations set a new course of direction. As noted earlier, all of the leaders in the examples had training and experience with the "meaningful change" process.

Case Study One: Heat from the Parent Company

A UK-based division of a global consumer products company was feeling the pressure to create a billion-dollar business out of a consistently profitable venture that had "plateaued." However, after three years of failing to gain market share, the leadership team was starting to feel the heat. They were painfully aware that their growth efforts lacked strategic coherence. They would add products or buy "growth" through acquisitions, but the lack of strategic integration into their core business created a string of failures.

Roger, their COO and chief architect of the initiatives, saw the writing on the wall and asked for an exit package.

The remaining team had finally faced the reality that there would be no "quick fixes." As the change conversation cascaded down into the organization, it also became clear that the employees had lost some faith in the executive team's ability to not just grow the organization but to grow those within it. The broader organization was also hoping for a more customer-centered enterprise, one that was not continually distracted with acquisitions and unproven product ventures.

Knowing this would be their last chance, the leadership team began to formulate a change journey that would build their internal customer capabilities more fully. They had some ideas on how that might evolve but committed to fully engaging the entire organization in the change process. The initial framing below signaled a new direction that the organization began to rally around.

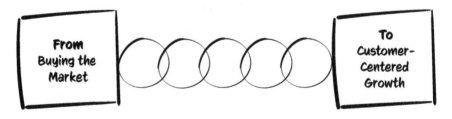

 Reflection question: *Would your larger organization benefit from a reframing of their overall purpose?*

Case Study Two: Somebody Help!

This case reveals how the FROM-TO meaningful change process can be scaled to smaller change efforts. In this case, a nursing leader, Anna, was conducting a feedback session with her team after lukewarm engagement survey results. The discussion seemed to hit a nerve when one nurse simply proclaimed: "We're in a helping profession but we don't help each other." Others jumped in and soon the notion of building a more "helping" culture between the nurses was gaining steam. However, one of the nurses chimed in that a "helping protocol" for nurses already existed but was not actively utilized. She further suggested they just dust it off and put some teeth into it.

Anna resisted the easy way out, especially after seeing too many of the other nursing protocols fall by the wayside. Anna continued the discussion to get below the surface and was rewarded with a vibrant and honest exchange of ideas. She started with a simple question that revealed elements of both the current (FROM) and desired future state (TO):

What is it about a "helping" culture that appeals to you?

Here's a sampling of responses:

- There are times when I want to ask for help but I know how busy everyone is.
- We've gotten used to being "Lone Rangers," taking care of our assigned patients only.
- In those rare instances when we do help each other, it feels great. It makes me feel like I am part of a team.
- There are definitely times where another set of hands or eyes should be our standard to ensure patient safety.
- I remember the previous protocol; it wasn't relevant to our situation.

The conversations continued, and Anna was able to find ways to stimulate even more conversation at the pre-shift huddles. The journey framing from "Lone Rangers" to "happy to help" captured the true sentiments of the group.

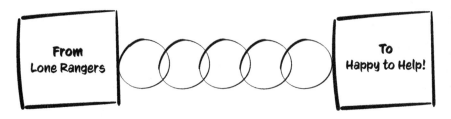

 Reflection question: *Is there a meaningful change initiative within your group that could have an "exponential" impact on the team culture?*

Case Study Three: The Purposeful School

The principal of a K–12 school faced a problem. As the students moved into high school, getting into a great college became the focus—the *only* focus. This obsession led to building the best possible resume with top grades, high test scores, and a range of activities to reveal the students' "great" character. It also led to higher levels of stress and burnout, as the students often struggled to meet these high expectations. This singular focus was also distorting what the principal, staff, and teachers felt was the true mission of the school:

Preparing students to lead in an increasingly challenging world.

After lots of conversation, they felt they were ready to go to the parents to start a new conversation. The hope was a return to a more balanced approach of developing the whole person and taking the pressure off of the college admissions game. This new focus would also emphasize developing leadership capabilities. This reorientation required some trade-offs; some of the time and focus on college admissions activities would give way to leadership development activities. As a result, they were prepared for pushback from parents but were ready for heartfelt discussion on a potential new journey that they were framing as follows:

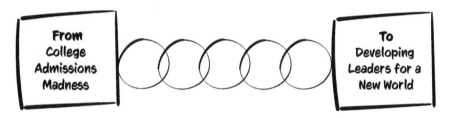

 Reflection question: *Do you work in a nonprofit or are you involved in a community organization that could benefit from a new direction?*

Case Study Four: Let's Think about This

A nonprofit was providing free counseling services to at-risk people in the community. During the pandemic, the counselors had to move their counseling services to an online video platform. At first it felt awkward, lacking the intimacy and connection of in-person interaction. However, over time, the "online skills" of the counselors grew, as did those of the clients. As life started to "normalize" after the COVID-19 vaccine became available, the executive director, Louise, was anxious to get back to normal as well. She sent out a note to counselors and clients with the good news that a future date would be established to bring the counseling services back in-house and in-person.

Unfortunately, for most, this was not good news.

Although some felt "stuck on Zoom," many had adapted to the online format and actually experienced some benefits from connecting from home and eliminating travel time. Louise's e-mail generated a ton of pushback. One of the program managers, Jordan, convinced her this presented an opportunity for a deeper discussion on how to best provide their services. Louise agreed. A survey and live feedback sessions revealed that both counselors and clients wanted to retain the use of the online format in combination with the traditional in-person process. A lot more discussion would be needed to figure out the different options, but there was great excitement about the new framing for the exploration:

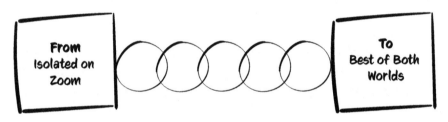

Reflection question: *How well does your organization leverage its "lessons learned" into new solutions?*

About the Authors

Mike Morrison, Ph.D., is the founder of the University of Toyota. His consulting and coaching work has taken him around the globe in service to a range of leading enterprises. He is the author of *Leading Through Meaning: A Philosophical Inquiry*, *The Other Side of the Card*, and *This is Not Working*. He continues to be a lifelong student and practitioner of leadership, culture development, and lean thinking. He has also served as a senior scientist for the Gallup Organization. He currently resides in Los Angeles with his wife, Kerry, and their three cats, Gus, Joni, and Angelina. Their adult children, Zack and Mackenzie, live in New York and Los Angeles, respectively.

 www.linkedin.com/in/mike-morrison-ph-d-580b0b14

Clint Kofford's career has demonstrated a commitment to creating meaningful change through innovative talent and leadership practices at organizations including the National Veterinary Associates, Johnson & Johnson, Nike, Mars, and the United States Olympic and Paralympic Committee. He is currently working on his doctorate at the University of Pennsylvania. The most important part of Clint's life is the time he spends with his family: his wife, Nancy, and his kids, David, Emma, Claire, and Jackson. As a family they enjoy serving in their church and community and boating on nearby lakes.

in www.linkedin.com/in/ckofford

Opportunities to Connect

If these ideas on *creating meaningful change* have resonated with you, we would love to continue the discussion and support you on your ongoing journey.

We have created a website (www.meaningfulchangebook.com) where you can find timely articles, "how-to" templates, and other supporting materials to keep the conversation going.

We can't wait to meet you!

Mike and Clint

Notes

1   John Gardner, "Personal Renewal" speech delivered to McKinsey & Company, Phoenix, AZ, November 10, 1990. https://www.pbs.org/johngardner/sections/writings_speech_1.html

2   Viktor E. Frankl, *Man's Search for Meaning* (Boston: Beacon Press, 1992), 98-101.

3   Frankl, *Man's Search for Meaning*, 77-78.

4   Frankl, *Man's Search for Meaning*, 36-37.

5   Frankl, *Man's Search for Meaning*, 108-112.

6   Martin Seligman, *Flourish: A Visionary New Understanding of Happiness and Well-being* (New York: Atria Books, 2012), 11-16.

7   Seligman, *Flourish*, 17-18.

8   The poet and plumber metaphor is attributed to James Marsh, Stanford professor in organizational development and author of *A Behavioral Theory of the Firm* (1963).

9   Gianpiero Petriglieri and Jennifer Petriglieri, "Can Business Schools Humanize Leadership?" *Academy of Management Learning & Education* 14, no. 4 (2015): 625-647.

10   G. Petriglieri and J. Petriglieri, *Academy of Management Learning & Education*, 625-647.

11   Jeroen Stouten, Denise M. Rousseau, and David De Cremer, "Successful Organizational Change: Integrating the Management Practice

and Scholarly Literatures," *Academy of Management Annals* 12. no. 2 (2018): 752-788.

12   Joseph Campbell, *The Hero with a Thousand Faces* (Princeton, NJ: Princeton University Press, 1973).

13   Tina Kiefer, "Understanding the Emotional Experience of Organizational Change: Evidence from a Merger," *Advances in Developing Human Resources* (2002): 39-61.

14   The University of Toyota's leadership development programming leveraged the "FROM-TO" framing to balance the limiting focus of an operations-oriented work culture.

15   Over 50 supporting frameworks guided the development process.

16   Ozen Asik-Dizdar and Ayla Esen, "Sensemaking at Work: Meaningful Work Experience for Individuals and Organizations," *International Journal of Organizational Analysis* 24, no. 1 (March 2016): 2-17.

17   Asik-Dizdar and Esen, *International Journal of Organizational Analysis,* 2-17.

18   Leonie Hallow, Alex Good, and Tiep Nguyen, "Effectiveness of Leadership Decision-Making in Complex Systems," *Systems* (February 2020): 1-21.

19   Catherine Travis, "Kind, Considerate, Thoughtful: A Semantic Analysis," *Lexikos* (Series 7: 1997): 130-152.

20   Karl Weick, Kathleen Sutcliffe, and David Obstfeld, "Organizing and the Process of Sensemaking," *Organization Science* 16, no. 4 (2005): 409-421.

21   Weick, Sutcliffe, and Obstfeld, *Organization Science* 16, no. 4 (2005): 409-421.

22   Andrew D. Brown, Ian Colville, and Annie Pye, "Making Sense of Sensemaking in Organization Studies," *Organization Studies* 36, no. 2 (2015): 265-277.

23   Ian Colville, Andrew Brown, and Annie Pye, "Simplexity:

Sensemaking, Organizing and Storytelling for our Time," *Human Relations Journal* 65, no. 1 (2011): 5-15.

24   Carol Dweck, "What Having a Growth Mindset Actually Means," *Harvard Business Review Articles* (January 17, 2016).

25   Dweck.

26   Nathanael Massey, "Humans May Be the Most Adaptive Species," *ClimateWire,* September 25, 2013.

27   Andrea E. Abele and Bogdan Wojciszke, "Communion from the Perspective of Self Versus Others," *Journal of Personality and Social Psychology* 93, no. 5 (December 2007): 751-63.

28   Marylene Gagne and Edward L. Deci, "Self-Determination Theory and Work Motivation," *Journal of Organizational Behavior* (2005): 331-362.

29   Carsten De Dreu and Aukje Nauta, "Self-Interest and Other-Orientation in Organizational Behavior: Implications for Job Performance, Prosocial Behavior, and Personal Initiative," *Journal of Applied Psychology* 94, no. 4 (2009): 913-926.

30   Di Fabio, Palazzeschi, and Bucci, "Gratitude in Organizations: A Contribution for Healthy Organizational Contexts," *Frontiers in Psychology Journal* (November 2017).

31   Di Fabio, Palazzeschi, Bucci, *Frontiers in Psychology Journal* (November 2017).

32   Daniel Kahneman and Jason Riis, "Living, and Thinking about It: Two Perspectives on Life," in *The Science of Well-Being*, ed. F.A. Huppert, N. Baylis, and B. Keverne (Oxford University Press, 2005), 285-304.

33   Daniel Kahneman, *Thinking Fast and Slow* (New York: Farrar, Straus and Giroux, 2011): 20-25

34   Kahneman, *Thinking Fast and Slow*, 20-25.

35   Michaéla C. Schippers and Niklas Ziegler, "Life Crafting as a Way

to Find Purpose and Meaning in Life," *Frontiers in Psychology Journal* (December 2019).

36　Ryan M. Niemiec, Tayyab Rashid, and Marcello Spinella, "Strong Mindfulness: Integrating Mindfulness and Character Strengths," *Journal of Mental Health Counseling* 34, no. 3 (July 2012): 240-253.

Made in the USA
Las Vegas, NV
02 December 2022

60909134R00066